UX Design

A field guide to process and methodology

for timeless user experience

STEVEN MILLER

Table of Contents

Introduction

UX has become a semi-household word; you practically hear it in everyday conversation and is all anyone in tech seems to want to talk about. Although the word, or juxtaposition of two letters if you choose to see it that way, gets flung around with the same effort used to breathe, many do not understand it. For many people who may want to get into the UX space, it is something designers say when they want to be high-sounding or push away the uninitiated. For some designers, the concept isn't all that clear; where exactly does clean design equal great UX? Are animations necessary for excellent UX? These are the two sides that usually present in UX conversations and I have considered both while writing this book.

I aim to change that with this book

UX is simply User Experience. I know it doesn't make complete sense, but abbreviations weren't created for the purpose of making sense as they are more about *snazziness* and ease. At this point, I should add a third group that will benefit from this book: UX design managers. My mission with this book is to produce designers by teaching the fundamentals in a straightforward manner—a surprisingly missing method in many books—and give managers a better grasp on how to lead teams. If you have picked up books that deal with UX as a method of thinking and practice but couldn't make sense of them because of an overabundance of theory without a clear path to hands-on application, then this book is an answer to your prayers. What you have in front of you isn't a book that is only aimed at getting you to enter the UX mentality or think like a designer. The goal is simple and straightforward: to teach you how to be a UX designer on your very first day. So expect practical lessons mixed in with theories that will keep you grounded in the discipline. The field of UX design is vast, and the resources available walk the plank of extreme theoretical principles and shortcuts that don't help a budding designer create an ingenious design by analyzing what is available.

I have tried to balance these two extremes here so you can be adequately armed to go out and be the best designer possible.

This book is not a survey of user experience or human-computer interaction. It isn't about human–computer interaction research or usability – these are touched on and expanded in individual sections, but they do not form the bulk of this book. This book is meant to be a how-to-do-it field guide and is intended to be a textbook and guide for aspiring practitioners and practitioners aiming to be rock-star designers.

The approach is practical; references only point to the science end of things while providing context to aid practice. This book is a great place of initiation into the world of UX so you get to talk like those who are veterans while learning to walk like they are. Anyone involved in or interested in gaining more knowledge about creating interaction designs that leads to quality user experience will benefit immensely from this book.

If you're reading this, chances are you work in a startup or hope to become an entrepreneur someday. Your role may have you working with usability analysts, software engineers, documentation specialists, programmers, systems analysts, graphic designers, marketing personnel, project managers and graphic designers – whatever the case, this book's approach will be valuable.

As you embark on this journey, I hope that you come away with invaluable knowledge that will shoot you through the roof of your career as you create amazing UX.

1

UX Design: Definition and Beyond

Don Norman coined the popular term user experience. We have him to thank for the ingenuity. Don came up with the term while he was vice president of the Advanced Technology Group at Apple in the 1990s. For anyone that has studied the evolution of computers, design, humankind, and the adoption of new tech, building systems in the 90s was hard work. There was a lot to grapple with, and the space was fairly new to them; a lot of what we have built on came from diligent exploration and championing of what was an unknown space. I am giving this brief background, so you understand what Don was grappling with at the time; the variables and uncertainties they had to test before stumbling on one usable formula.

"I thought human interface and usability were too narrow. I wanted to cover all aspects of the person's experience with the system, including industrial design graphics, the interface, the physical interaction, and the manual," Don said when asked about the term he was waving around. It must have seemed crazy an idea for people back then because of the nature of what he was describing. How on earth do you cram all those disciplines into one field and not expect disaster? Of course, there were skeptics, there are always skeptics when it comes to doing stuff no one has done before, but Don continued straight for what he had envisioned.

Since then, the term has spread widely. Unfortunately, this spread isn't all good. The potency of the meaning behind UX is gradually being lost in a sea of mindless buzz. To this devaluation of the field, Don, like all good visionaries, has a response in hand: "It's easy enough to let the term *UX* roll off the tongue, but many people lack an appreciation of what it means to deliver the broader aspects of UX, instead of taking a narrow approach and considering only one or two elements."

What are these broader aspects, and why do they matter? Interesting question, you ask. These encompassing discipline, how they weave in and out, their pertinence, and the field's future is what we would consider throughout this book. Buckle up.

Broadly considering a user's lifestyle in the context of how a service or system is presented is necessary towards improving user experience.

Top-notch consideration for user experience is especially important and pertinent when building digital services, although this way of thinking has spread into other sectors. It is critical to note that, although digital media takes center stage in a lot of UX discussions, it is still very much important and being implemented in other aspects of user servicing industries. Here's an example, think of a well-known hotel, anyone would do. Why do you think they have maintained a name over the years? Why do people able to afford it prefer these hotels to others? I can bet you that their service is the To the end-user (or customer), the UX you provide will reflect their perceived experience with your brand, whether dealing with your company online, via a mobile app, or talking to your call center.

UX embraces a multidisciplinary approach: the method of using multiple perspectives when tackling a design issue leads to the best outcomes. It incorporates contributions from various disciplines, including but not limited to:

- computer science

- psychology

- sociology

- industrial design

- anthropology

- interaction design

- graphic design

- human factors engineering

- cognitive science

As a matter of broad strokes, UX brings together all these elements and cuts across digital and non-digital experiences. This approach makes a logical point when considering the varying perspectives around definitions in different sectors: when defining what a customer is can cause confusion among industries; the marketing department might define customer experience differently from, say, an industrial designer. Both may be correct based on what they know and goals. Most times, design tailored for non-digital user-product experiences is called experience design, while the famous cousin of the two is called customer experience. The latter is sometimes used to refer to the sum total of interactions a person has with an organization/brand/startup.

A large chunk of focus in this book will be on a process that can be implemented across your projects, thereby birthing a seamless interaction between user and product. It is my assumption that your projects, products if you will, are digital, although the UX design process as examined and presented here can also be applied to effectively design offline products and services. More than assessing a product's ease of use, the philosophy guiding the course of UX puts the end-users needs at the center of the design and development process. This effectively sweeps away the assumption, by most people, that the discipline only covers interface design and digital products. The field is about understanding then prioritizing user needs before, during, and after any interaction a user has with a company, which isn't limited to the pixelated walls of a digital service.

This unsurprisingly switches the traditional IT approach where technology drives decisions. More often than not, technology projects have failed because they haven't been designed with a user in mind. They haven't been infused with enough information guided by research to anticipate the type of person that will ultimately use the product. Neither is the context of usage considered. So, if you have ever wondered why technology projects have failed in the past despite having ridiculous sell points and potential, look no further. Building without the ability to predict or care for what the user may want and how to get it to them will ultimately lead to failure.

What constitutes an experience?

I get this question a lot when I teach, or I simply bring it up to put certain things in a useful context. A memorable experience differs from one person to the next because we have varying interests and filters through which we view life. What I hold as a great experience may not make your list. This is all true, but there is usually a unifying thread that links and binds all great experiences. It is inbuilt in each and everyone, but there is a formula to it. The secret is that great experiences answer a question. They fulfill a need, an order, a gap if you will. Think of all the big-name brands you have interacted with or know about because of the news; what do they do? They create experiences by filling a need/want.

Several factors affect the overall experience a user has with a product, system, service, or person and some of them are:

- Usefulness: How useful is the product/service? Does it solve a big problem? Does it serve a clear purpose?

- Usability: How easy is it to navigate? Are some elements useful, or do they encumber and make it difficult for the user to accomplish tasks?

- Learnability: Is it intuitive? How easy can a new user pick it up? How steep is the learning curve?

- Aesthetics: How high is the interface's appeal? Is there a deliberateness behind color choices and structure?

- Emotions: What emotions would you want to evoke in the user? Are the current assembled elements achieving this goal? What lasting effect do you want the user to leave with?

When you consider this range of potential influences, it's easy to see why many disciplines come together to design and deliver a holistic UX. Each element answers key aspects that guide the design of a truly excellent experience for the user. Some colors are more memorable than others; some evoke a sour reaction, while others give off a certain vibrance, which all feed into the process.

Methodology

In the arena of UX, we examine users' needs. This shouldn't be a strange concept for you at this point, but what you probably don't know is the methodology guiding it. The needs of the user are examined using a series of contextual methods known as a User-centered Design (UCD) methodology. UCD is a framework that enables UX designers to engage with and listen to users for the sake of understanding what they want. You really don't want to be guessing what users want.

UCD takes on an approach that considers the user's needs first and foremost throughout the design and development process so as to ensure that the product doesn't miss anything. UCD practices help designers generate designs/schemes that take on a more integrated UX approach in the overall system. Often, I hear people say they lack time to involve users, and I am not surprised when most of these projects implode or fail to reach heights predicted and imagined. The earlier you bring on users or include them in the scheme of the things to evaluate your designs, the more likely your chances to succeed. The opposite is also true: keeping users out or not considering them will always have you running back to the drawing board to rework what you set out to build. I feel I should add this, the bigger your project, the more cost you will incur by doing things this way. You will save money and time if you take action and step in early, listen and evaluate feedback from end-users, get a feel for what the product will mean to them, and ways to make it better way before any final decisions are made. This step is essential to success.

UCD takes an intuitive approach: from the research phase where understanding the problem being solved and the context it is to be used in, followed by interpreting insights; making sense of data gleaned from listening to users, then the concept stage; prototyping, sketching, iterating designs, and getting more user feedback as you move to towards a final product. The final phase is implementation, creating the design experience by monitoring and making changes over the lifetime of the product/service.

Many of the methods commonly used in a UX process are qualitative in nature rather than quantitative. Later on, when we take a look at the behavior, you will see how qualitative research looks at users' unfiltered behaviors in order to gain an in-depth and precise understanding of the decision-making process.

Quantitative research is often done through large-scale market surveys that cover big sample sizes – usually involving thousands of participants. This research focuses on mass data collection and analyzing its themes with the aim of gleaning insights into assumptions surrounding human behavior. Interestingly, when viewed through the lens of statistics, quantitative research gives a better sense of where, when, and what, which are motivators and attitudes crucial to understanding our leanings. Usually, qualitative research requires a much smaller sample size than its data-driven counterpart. This is good news as insights collected from a few users are not hard to obtain and will improve your approach to work if gathered early and often as work progresses. Understanding behavior is the first step toward changing or influencing if you will, the way users perform tasks. You have an incredible amount of control over how a user of your product reacts or doesn't react during interactions.

A Balanced Approach to Solving Problems

In UX, we're led by the desires of the user. This culture is a way of driving the creation of products and services, but this is counterbalanced by asking feasibility and viability questions. Remember, users don't have all the answers; while they're great for informing and testing our design concepts, they should never be the sole basis of any business decision. Questions are meant to guide them toward putting their thought together in a way that would help you build. If left on their own without questions as a form of structure, users may very well give vague answers or not contribute anything meaningful at all. It is no fault of the user when this happens. It is yours. Users know what they want but may not be able to communicate it clearly and effectively; that is your job. Learn to use questions that lead and draw out actionable answers.

Once insights into our target users are gathered, overall feasibility and viability must be reviewed and assessed in light of deliverables; what the business can actually deliver on. Most successful product designs come from an understanding of the balance between users,

Steven Miller

needs, and the business, which means taking the UX path requires a thorough understanding of the business landscape, a larger scope when compared to whatever project you are working on. Design thinking is an overall process that consists of rapidly coming up with ideas, testing them, and getting feedback from real users while simultaneously refining your approach. This is the essence of UX.

This often means communicating across different disciplines—branding, psychology, product management, marketing—in order to actualize desired outcomes. UCD methods have long been a foundation to design thinking as it is the plumb that guides the builder.

In easy to digest bullet points, design thinking is essentially about:

- being human-centered, which draws on empathy and understanding the user

- Continuous ideation calls on your capacity to generate ideas, test them out, flip them upside down and go through iterations until you find one worthy of pursuing.

- The employment of prototypes as a tangible way to feel through design problems and solution ideas; prototyping calls for input from users if effective reiterations are ever going to happen.

Following UCD principles doesn't mean that the user controls what happens at the of the day. No. Rather than the user dictating outcomes, the feedback given helps you to think about the problem while sponsoring your ideas to take form and flight. It is possible that this approach is different from what you imagined made up a UX approach, but I hope it reveals how you can mix in your ideas with user feedback in order to attain the best-structured design solution. Exposure to products and services across various areas of an organization helps us to design end-to-end experiences that are an unforgettable pleasure to use, and you may also identify areas where business costs can be reduced. Adopting this plan of attack on your projects will guarantee that you're pulling your ideas together quickly, making informed choices, evaluating and reviewing your ideas with others, and gathering feedback early and often from the product's end-users. All this works to ensure that you'll succeed once you've gone live.

Put yourself in the user's shoes.

Two factors essential to a successful UX approach are:

- consider the person will eventually interact with your product

- consider the context the product might be used in

Ultimately, everything boils down to having empathy. Quite often, I find myself thinking: How would my parents react to this product? To me, they represent everyday users and are a good litmus test for whether my designs will be well-received by a broader audience. My parents, probably like yours too, are part of the majority of people not working in IT or any technical industry: they are neither tech-savvy or understand its intricate nature but find themselves being pushed into the digital world by companies that are looking for ways to service clients. Like most users I've had the opportunity of talking to, my parents hesitate when they are confronted with new technology for the first time. Yours are probably the same way too. I don't think there are a lot of parents that are eager to jump in blindfolded; they worry about breaking something by pressing the wrong button. If we are to collect all the stories of fear and trepidation exhibited by parents and people from an older generation, books will be the result.

Here's what I've learned, users do a range of crazy, unexpected things with the interfaces we design, and design patterns we believe are easy to understand are sometimes unclear. Over the years, I've listened as users blame themselves when they find a product difficult to use. They shrug and convince themselves that they will get used to it. This resignation has been observed and reported for years now within the UX industry, but it still surprises me when this helplessness shows up in our user-focused research. This learned behavior should ideally have been dealt with, seeing as it is not new behavior for UX designers, but it sadly remains and shows up ever so often.

In your design work, it's essential to have empathy for the end-users of your product, and this is more easily achieved working in the UX field than you might think. You'll often come up against regular reality checks. Ultimately, it's not the user's fault if they can't make a system work; it is our responsibility as designers to get it right for them and to make it as easy as possible for them to perform the tasks they want to do.

Involving Users Helps You to Perfect Your Product

So how do these reality checks come about? Well, considering how your users will deal with what you're creating and exposing a project to feedback early and often throughout the design process is a good start. No matter how well you think you know the mindset of those that will eventually use a system, we must always take heed that we are not our users. Even after years of watching users in testing sessions, there is always something that surprises me, something new I learn, or something unexpected. You need to watch your users, engage with them, and persuade them to use your designs so that you can learn how they think and behave. It enables you to know them a little better and understand the context under which they're using your product. Some of the design projects I've worked on have required me to go into users' homes or workplaces to gain a sense of how they live and work. This has helped me to empathize with contexts of use I may be unfamiliar with, such as designing health-related devices for the elderly or chronically ill or understanding how specialist workers do their job. Seeing users interact with initial design concepts helps to evolve our design thinking and improve our output. Considering how to involve users in your design process can be a daunting process. Throughout this book, I'll point out situations where you can consider users' input and offer advice on techniques at different stages of the UX process. I'll provide practical ways to gather feedback rather than focus on lengthy engagement models. As is often cited in the UX field, some user engagement is better than no user engagement. Bringing in the user in the design process is the best way to double-check that your approach is solving the design issue at hand. It can be tricky to deliver a great experience—but all the best experiences are well thought out and pre-engineered; they don't just happen by accident.

Good and Bad User Experiences

So what are the most incredible and worst experiences you've ever had? I'll bet that more comes to mind about an actual company or situation than just one narrow aspect of the experience itself. It covers the way people feel about an experience and how satisfied they are when using it. It is often unexpected factors that have the biggest impact. This is important when solving design problems: people notice small details. So that's the good experience; what about the bad? Well, my worst user experience involved a cheap plastic watch that I bought while my regular watch is being repaired. My life is dictated by the clock, and the thought of being without a wristwatch for four whole months was not an option I was going to entertain. Sure, it's the twenty-first century, and like everyone else, I have a phone that displays the time and is always in reach. I just like glancing at my wrist to find out the time! This well-known brand makes plastic Swiss watches that are cheap, fun, and loud in design; however, it was only after buying the watch I realized it was going to prove frustrating in one critical way: its inability to show the time clearly. Showing the time is the central reason a watch exists. It seems the design team for this particular watch forgot some really basic factors, namely, to ensure the hour, minute, and second hands can be easily distinguished. Maybe there was a legitimate reason this oversight occurred, but, ultimately, as the user of the watch, I don't care much about any behind-the-scenes motivations. All I know is that I have trouble telling the time on it, and as a result, I'll never buy another watch like this again. Interestingly, my usual behavior of looking at my wrist when I need to know the time has changed with the passing of the months. Now I'm more likely to check my phone or my computer if I happen to be sitting at my desk. As a result, I am losing the reliance I once had on my watch. This demonstrates how design has influenced my overall experience to such a degree that it has changed my behavior. It also illustrates what to be on the lookout for in design research. Shortcuts and workarounds that users might take tell us there's an element they're encountering that needs to be examined. This is avoidance behavior. We should home in on these alerts, as they provide hints to help us refashion a product, service, or system. Another important point worthy of note is the balance between utility and aesthetics. Both factors are important, but, in the end, if some item looks cool but is fairly useless, your users will soon lose interest. In my case, the watch sure is pretty, but my old one will be back in a month—at which point this watch will be retired to my daughter's jewelry box. She's three years old, so being unable to read the time won't bother her too much just yet!

I trust these examples show that we should be concerned with the opinions of our end-users. Experiences birth memories for people, and there is a benefit in creating positive experiences and unforgettable memories for customers as opposed to negative ones. At the heart of it, negative experiences cost money, as angry customers are more likely to adopt another brand. Customers who are happy with you, on the other hand, will refer your brand to others and speak volumes about the experiences they have had with it should be your goal. In what is becoming a more and more competitive landscape, the thoughts, feelings, impressions, and experiences of users count. Impacts on Customer Loyalty Research has shown that companies that ensure that certain tasks require minimal effort from the customer are more likely to see greater customer loyalty.

Simplifying the interactions that users have with your brand has clear positive benefits. Customers that move from one brand to another cost companies money; it is easier to try to please a difficult customer than find a new one in a competitive market. So, how easy is it to do business with your company/client's company? You need to ask yourself this when looking at the overall UX of the products you're designing. What makes a great experience? When creating an experience for your users, think about what might make their lives that little bit easier, saving them time and effort. If you start by defining the experience you want your users to have with your product, the rest will follow. Why? Because happy users are loyal users, it's that simple. Great experiences differ for everyone, and there is often much banter about whether you can engineer an experience at all. What we do know is that as designers, we can manipulate a situation through our craft because our designs can influence a user's behavior.

Your users will teach you a lot if you pay attention! Listen intently. Observe without blinking. Take note of every little feedback you get. This seemingly unimportant information is the best way to learn; unwittingly, they are imparting to you what makes a great user experience for them. Never forget that you are designing for them. The popular platitude, *the customer is always right comes* to bear heavily in this field. Listening to your customers and adopting what they tell you will undoubtedly set you on the path to a great user experience.

In this chapter, we examined UX and noted factors that make a good or bad experience. You also learned what it means to focus on the UX of a system, how to put the user into your plans when designing and why this approach pays in the long run. To be certain we are on the wavelength, I have made a compressed list of things you should know before going to the next chapter. If you find your knowledge shaky in an area, I encourage you to backtrack and learn it down pat.

Here's a laundry list of what you should know at this point:

- UX as a field of design can be viewed as the collection of a series of interactions a person has with a service or organization.

- It concentrates on the end-users of the product, envisioning problems they may encounter, how to solve them and get the best experience possible across through concise problem-solving principles.

- UX takes on several disciplines, bringing to bear their different perspectives and approaches to problem-solving.

- UX thrives on a balanced approach of desirability, feasibility, and viability. What does the user want answers the question of desirability. Can it be done given the available resources on hand, answers feasibility. Does it make sense for the business, service, or app, answers the question on viability. This pipeline process ensures that you come out with solid, tailor-made solutions that cater to your customers and business.

2

Much ado about UX

If you are new to user experience, you may have noticed that the word *user* tends to be thrown around a lot. You will hear *user-centered design, user goals, user journeys*, and, of course, "user experience." It would seem that the user is highly prioritized within the field of UX. But even within UX, the user is often neglected. Consider the following statement: A user is a person having an experience. The statement is so sparse that it sounds whimsical. Yet, this basic idea is at the core of what a user is. Over time, an artifice forms around this definition, complicating its discourse and draining its value. What was once a simple idea complicating its discourse and draining its value? What was once a simple idea branches off into multiple directions, like a river spreading across a delta. You can surround it with marketing flourishes or embellish it with academic phraseology, but the fundamental idea remains: You must have a user to have an experience, and you must have an experience to have a user. The two are inseparable.

You might see yourself as a potential user when creating an experience, such as a website or an app. For instance, your team may create a gourmet cooking app full of tasty recipes. You think, "I love food, and I know a lot about gourmet cooking." But, even though you may use an app, you are still not the user —you are the creator using the app. Even experienced designers sometimes make this mistake.

Consider the following hypothetical example: Fishes'R'Us wants to create an iPhone app that helps users understand how to cook seafood. You love seafood and cook it often; therefore, you believe you are a user. Sounds logical enough, yes? However, a problem arises in following such logic because, even though you may be a member of the target audience, your mere involvement in the project affects your objectivity. This is best demonstrated by taking the previous example and adding a bit of background information: Fishes'R'Us wants to create an iPhone app [and is paying you to provide a solution] that helps users [who may know more or less than you do] understand how to cook seafood. You love seafood and cook it often [and you already know how the app works, what it offers, and what it does not]… Do you still believe you are a user? You have a vested interest in designing an experience. You want your client to be satisfied, your company to be successful, and your team to be happy. These concerns can affect your objectivity. They often do. Perhaps your client's desire to create an app is misguided, and the app should instead be a website, a Facebook page, or a podcast. Perhaps your company wants to *wow* the client and recommends unnecessary features and functionality. Perhaps you want to be seen as a team player and support your team's cutting-edge ideas. These desires and concerns are understandable, and some may even be admirable. However, the cruel reality is that users do not share these concerns. Users do not know your client, your team, or you. They do not care about your project as much as you do—if they do at all. They cast their attention toward their own lives, their own needs, and their own desires. Their thoughts are filled with private concerns about their jobs and families, as well as their own projects, ranging from the banality of mowing lawns to the excitement of planning vacations. You may eventually lure users into caring about the experiences you create, but a user's biases and interests will always differ from your own. He or she may learn to love your creation, and he or she may eventually use it every hour of every day, but—right now, at this moment—you are not that person.

You are not the user

Competing with everything is an antithetical statement for many project teams. As a member of a project team, we are focused on the act of creation. We know that we compete within market segments: Brand A is better than Brand B, App #1 offers more than App #2, etc. Yet, we are often far less honest with ourselves about how small of an impact our creations make on users' lives. Yes, it would be wonderful if users loved our project as much as we do. But they do not. They do not care if our app sells. They do not care about our industry. They do not care about you or me. Embrace, Not Accommodate Users do care about themselves. They seek solutions to their needs. Needs range from locating emergency assistance to satisfying idle curiosity. Necessity. Utility. Entertainment. Companionship. Advice. You name it. Reasons span the vital to the mundane and are only limited by a user's imagination, circumstance, and attention. However, every reason shares a single, common attribute: users would rather embrace a solution than accommodate it. Close your eyes and try to bring to mind the last time you were required to do something unpleasant, such as fill out a tax return form. You had to find the correct documents. You had to calculate the precise totals. You had to file by a specific date. None of this was likely done joyfully—you accommodated. Now, try to recall a pleasant situation, such as eating a bowl of salted caramel ice cream. You may have considered consuming a bowl of broccoli, gobbling down a plate of pinto beans, or devouring a saucer of semolina, but ultimately you chose what you wanted to experience. You did not accommodate a bowl of ice cream—you embraced it.

How do we create experiences that users will embrace? We already have the answer: users embrace what they willingly choose above all else—what they believe will best meet their own needs. If a user seeks information, she will choose what she believes is the most informative. If a user seeks entertainment, he will choose what he believes is the most entertaining. If they are unable to find what they need, they may accommodate a solution, but that solution will never take home a gold medal. It only temporarily satisfies until a stronger competitor enters the marketplace.

Designing experiences often feels like playing a never-ending game, fraught with high hurdles to jump and selfish users to satisfy. Although these challenges are daunting, you are no more disadvantaged than anyone else. Each experience competes with all others. User experience is a broad but equal playing field that competes with all others. User experience is a broad but equal playing field, daring all players to strive for greater knowledge and inspiring all audiences to seek out better experiences.

The user begins our journey at the first intersection along the road, where her path and ours meet. After all, she comes from somewhere else. She has walked other roads before ours. When we meet the user at this crossroad, she either decides to join us or ignore us. More often than not, she fails to even take notice—many distractions compete for her attention. We want to know where the user was before we met her. We want to know her context. The user's context is arguably the most important part of a user's journey, for it often determines which path she will take next. If the user comes from a context applicable to the path we constructed, she may join us; if not, she will likely take another route. For instance, buying a plane ticket online would be applicable in the context of planning a vacation, whereas it rarely would be in the context of planning a meal.

With a bit of coaxing, the user elects to travel down our road. Her journey with us will continue or end at the next intersection. For instance, she will reach a crossroad where she will debate buying from us. We can guide the user to a preferred path if we know where they are within the journey. If they are ready to learn, then we should sit to eat.

If our research is correct (and with a bit of luck), we can anticipate the intersections, points of interest, and dead ends along a user's journey. We design accordingly. Each design decision becomes a result of the user's goals. If we know that users first search for a product, we should direct our awareness-building efforts toward search engine marketing and optimization. If we believe users make purchase decisions only after an app's download, we should focus on post-installation conversion. If we understand that users abandon their accounts within 90 days, we should foster retention within the first few months of use. Within 90 days, we should foster retention within the first few months of use. Despite their many similarities, a marathon full of drunk runners and the journey of users do differ in at least one key way: running a marathon is a solo act driven by the skill and passion of an individual. In contrast, a user journey is a partnership between a user and a designer, driven by the designer's empathy for the user and an understanding of the user's goals. The more you understand a user's goals, the greater the chances are that you will reach yours as well. A user journey is merely the road map to achieve them. Place yourself in the user's shoes and design the paths that he or she will travel. It is the only way to win. So, open a bottle of your favorite wine, crack open a few oysters, and sizzle up some steak—you have a marathon to run.

Head-to-head, a battle between a single Maus and a single Sherman would certainly favor the Germans. The American tank's simplicity was both its weakness and its strength because wars are not won in single tank duels—they are won by design.

What does this decades-old example teach us about design? Complex designs are hard to build and even harder to maintain, be it a World War II tank or tomorrow's mobile app. No design exists in a vacuum. Each one is affected by all the others, and each one is only a small part of a greater system. Direct comparisons of competing products lead us into a never-ending arms race of features. Like a pair of dueling tanks, a single comparison may favor a complex solution over a simple one, but we must consider the entirety of a user's experience to understand which product will ultimately win.

Who is our user?

What is she attempting to do? When does she do it? How is she currently coping without our product? Why is our solution better than the second-best alternative? The wreckage of feature-rich products litters software history—Microsoft Bob, Google Lively, iTunes Ping, to name but a few. When we continually add to our creations, we weigh them down with complexity. We create complexity through the act of creation itself. It comes in the form of ideas, budgets, schedules, briefs, proposals, presentations, screens, gestures, web services, repositories, databases, scripts, classes, structures, and bug reports.

We roll out our software and hope it survives among the thousands of other experiences competing for our users' attention. Yet, complexity obliges us to focus our efforts on the construction and maintenance of the software itself instead of the experiences it creates. We lose sight of our objectives as we pursue the grand, the expansive, and the robust. Features break. Support fails.

Team members leave. Such flare-ups and conflicts divert us from our one true goal: we wish to fulfill a user's need in the simplest possible way. Let's look at three methods to defeat complexity.

In the story of Adam and Eve, a serpent tempted Eve to take a bite from the forbidden fruit. Eve could have been tempted by any number of distractions, ranging from harp lessons to finding sunblock. Yet, a talking snake grabbed her attention. The snake offered Eve knowledge. Eve accepted, and she and Adam were kicked out of Eden. From a user experience perspective, we cannot blame Eve. She is our user.

Users always crave knowledge, especially when they are tempted by something new and exciting. Think of the countless times you've ventured online to buy a gift, only to be derailed by a *BuzzFeed* article. We could easily blame the snake, but he is only partially to blame. The snake merely directs Eve toward the problem. He is not the problem itself. The problem is the forbidden fruit.

Remove the fruit, and the problem is solved. Adam and Eve lounge around for eternity, occasionally striking a pose for a Michelangelo fresco. Like the removal of the forbidden fruit from the Garden of Eden, we, too, can remove a distraction from our creation before it becomes a problem. People will not get themselves in trouble if you take away the opportunity to do so. Applications already do a great deal of work on behalf of users. Users do not need to pick the cell towers through which their calls are routed. They do not need to tell a website to encrypt their passwords. They do not need to translate video game moves into machine code. Why should users need to press a button?

3

UX DESIGN: FUNDAMENTALS

Defining UX principles can be a bit like battling a hydra. You tackle one principle, wait a short while, and two or more additional principles pop up in its place. It is a never-ending battle. Intriguing blog posts, inspiring speeches, and contentious Twitter spats reshape our understanding of UX on a near-daily basis. However, some principles do endure. This part of the book takes on the Herculean, and perhaps foolhardy, task of defining a core set of UX principles. The list is by no means exhaustive. A quick Google search of UX principles will return a long list of complementary approaches. The following principles were selected to represent the enduring concepts shared among many strategies to user experience design and research. User experience can first appear to be a giant, scary monster of rules, contradictions, and dilemmas. While partially true, it is a monster easily tamed. We tackle one principle at a time, sear it into our memories, and become heroes to the users of what we create.

Design Thinking and the User-Centered Approach

When it comes to proper design documentation, practice and theory are two rather distinct themes. The question you may often find yourself asking, though, is *How does it all work in practice? What does this look like?* We are all aware, for the most part, of the basic tenets governing user-centered design: we know the different research methods, everything about the prototyping stage, as well as the tedious but important process of documenting practices in our rich methodological environments.

Simply put, it all hinges on tailoring documentation to be complementary rather than supplementary to the design process. Before getting into detail, it might help to take a quick bird's eye view of the documentation process during product design and development. Just below, I've given a practical explanation of how every step of design documentation leads to another:

- During the initial phase of defining the product, you're brainstorming the product and how to execute the project at an optimal level with all necessary stakeholders. This may result in a project kickoff plan, a lean canvas, and a collection of early mockups and concept maps of your intended design.

- Diving into research, your team refines assumptions and fills in the blanks. This stage varies based on timing, knowledge, complexity of the product, resources, and several other factors. Generally speaking, however, it is an excellent idea to build from customer surveys in tandem with the market and competitive analyses. If you have an existing product, reviewing user tests, heuristics, analytics data, and product context is also beneficial.

  In an analysis, the product marketing data gleaned so far provides the foundation for experience maps, personas, and requirements documents such as prioritized feature user-task matrices and spreadsheets. Here the product definition, product priorities, and product plan have been defined and are ready for more rounded design deliverables. Sketches and diagrams are also likely continuously being generated throughout this time.

From this, scenarios, concept maps, and mockups may be created, leading into the design phase. Standard documentation includes sketches, wireframes, prototypes, task-flow diagrams, and design specifications. Here's an example, competitive analysis and personas created during research and analysis contribute to the mockups, concept maps, and scenarios. These pieces, in turn, influence inter-

...wate and advanced deliverables such as storyboards, wireframes, and super-detailed mockups. There exist companies that treat the Research, Analysis, and Design phase as one extensive process. During implementation, design and code assets are put together to create a product that follows, to the letter, the product design specifications outlined.

After the launch of the live product, feedback data such as bug reports, support tickets, and other pertinent analytics continue to propel product refinement through several upgrades, overhauls, or iterations. With the system in production mode, data should continually be generated and monitored in the form of analytics and reports to ensure unstoppable success. Let us take a look at guidelines to keep in mind as you employ design thinking with the user as your focus:

Understanding the Product You Want to Build

According to Smashing Magazine, you need to bring in activities that highlight the best design solutions, business requirements, and user needs when you come to this stage. Before you decide to build a product, you need to get under the skin of the context of its existence: Why should users, stakeholders, the company, and designers even care about running to the finish line with your idea? The keyword to note here is activities because while documents like the Business Model Canvas and Lean Canvas are essential, you need to energize stakeholders — otherwise, you just have a bunch of expensive people talking about things everyone is already familiar with. These activities invite collaboration and highly effective:

- Stakeholder interviews — You can delegate each team member to interview at most three stakeholders. Questions to be asked should revolve around: How will the product make customers feel? What should they do? Recording how stakeholders believe customers will think, feel, and do, you're setting a benchmark to compare against usability testing and user analysis.

- Good Things Comes in 8s — Collect some markers and ask team members to sketch 8 product or feature ideas in 5 minutes. Have everyone score each picture, and you'll suddenly start to see trends and preferences emerge.

- Requirements workshops — Invite stakeholders, put them in the same room, discuss the plan you have, then get them to discuss how each concept you bring up feeds into technical requirements and product design. It wouldn't be a bad idea to begin with a blank Business Model Canvas or Lean Canvas. Get your team involved in filling the canvas.

Designing the Product

Once you have a sense of the product's purpose, your main goal is to build a prototype. Whether your team likes to draw on scrap paper, create high or low fidelity wireframes, you should ultimately end up with a functional product. The unique thing about this stage is that for a large section of the deliverables, the documentation is hidden in the design. Cennydd Bowles, Design Manager at Twitter, says that the product team should, as a necessity, research two iterations ahead, design one ahead, and review the previous iteration. If you're planning to stay Agile, he advises diving straight into low fidelity prototypes as a prioritization method of interactions over processes. Although, if you want to get a bit more detailed and still maintain a somewhat lightweight build, you can start with concept maps or sketches, then redesign to low-fidelity wireframes, and finally create a high-fidelity prototype. Your method matters little in this; only make sure you test with stakeholders and users. If the budget and timing allow for it, you can also build experience maps to highlight where the product meets or fails users' needs and task models to give insight into activities users undergo to achieve their goals. While these aren't an integral part of the design, they act as complementary because you also need to understand precisely where your product fits into your mind and market. As a sort of spice, Yelp takes their design stage a step further by creating a style guide that includes standard lines of code, allowing the documentation to be built into the product literally.

Building And Launching The Product

At the start of the heavy technical lifting, it's vital to create documentation that helps you see the overarching vision. Specific needs may change as you refine the product, but your documentation should aid in your understanding of priorities as your product goes into the world.

Building a product road map helps you visualize and shows user stories. Interestingly, this helps prioritize the features you'll create to satisfy them. Sometimes, specific dates may be added to the roadmap so that it also works as a timeline. The elegance of the roadmap is that it helps you prioritize what you're building, making it complementary to the how scheme defined by your product needs and technical specifications.

To help decide features, you can use the Kano Model to evaluate them in 3 categories:

- Primary Attributes: These are absolutely required just for the product to work. For example, a laptop's fundamental attribute is the mouse or keyboard.

- Performance Attributes: These can be compared with different products as a KPI. For instance, a laptop is judged on

CPU speed and hard drive space since people tend to prefer fast computers that can store large amounts of information.

- Delightful Attributes — These attributes are subjective depending on customer preferences. For instance, the Macbook Air is extremely smooth to the touch. The right user would find it a great selling point while others may remain unimpressed.

Metrics Monitoring

As you build your product, remember that the documentation also needs to continue tracking sales and pertinent KPIs. After all, you can't upgrade the product if you have no knowledge of what metrics you want to optimize. Dave Daniels, Founder of LaunchClinic, says that you write down the launch goals and verify that you have the correct tools to document progress. Making use of metrics systems and bug reporting software, you can set up continuous reports to keep tabs in the first few weeks of launch and beyond. Meanwhile, on the customer side, you can also partition users and send them custom surveys to gauge where you may want to redesign. At Spotify, the iteration phase is usually the longest stage of the product development process. The team implements current metrics and prioritization matrix to weigh the benefits vs. effort of improving certain products beyond their local maximum.

Product Definition

The Product Definition phase creates the stage for the success or failure of your product; not paying proper attention to or completing this phase will leave you, your team, and the product in perpetual darkness. The arch-enemy of product development, after all, is ambiguity and untested assumptions. In the first phase of product design, your answers will come from brainstorming sessions and execution at the highest level with all stakeholders. This may result in a project kickoff plan, a lean canvas, and a collection of rough sketches of what you're trying to build. An accepted definition of a product is anything that can be offered to a market to service a need. If you've worked on products before, this definition should already be familiar. You also know that no matter how simple that objective might appear, making products market fit is a tricky business— they are, after all, created for people — and many products don't get this quite right.

Mark Curphey, the former Principal Group Manager at Microsoft, says the concept of the totality of the product is just one way of thinking about these needs. Take a supermarket canned soup, for example, it is more than just liquid in a tin can; the entire product includes the soup, the can label, the store display, and the store's hygiene. To help you better understand the tangible and intangible aspects of a product, here's a breakdown of the product into three levels:

- Core Product: This is the benefit(s) a consumer gains when purchasing a product. To help you understand it better, here is an example: the core product of a bed is sleep, not the mattress; everything else is built around this core.

- Augmented Product — This represents extra benefits and services linked with the actual product, for which consumers may pay a premium. The augmented product gives you the option to tailor the core or existing product to individual consumers. For example, IBM's success was basically due to its sophisticated software and after-sale services, the up-sale of other services, not the development of more cutting-edge computers.

- Actual Product — This is what we usually consider the physical product. Its goal is to deliver on the benefits preached by the core product being offered. Actual products may have as much as five characteristics tied to styling, brand, quality level, packaging, and features.

Because products are ultimately multidimensional, a structured product definition process is needed so that you can consider the physical, emotional as well as supplemental parts of the product. The lean canvas and project kickoff examines how and why consumers may be inclined to buy your product/patronize you, while rough sketching helps you bring those ideas to life.

The Kickoff Meeting

The kickoff meeting extensively covers the high-level outline of the purpose of the product, who is involved in designing and eventually developing a product, how they'll integrate nicely, stay up-to-date on the progress, and what the intended success metrics will become. The process is becoming much shorter as teams become more nimble and projects leaner, and the documentation can be presented in a document, project management software, or a wiki page. I'll go over how to prepare and conduct a kickoff as well as some general guiding principles.

Planning for the Kickoff

A project's kickoff is the equivalent of a grand opening. It brings all the key players together in one moment under one common theme and sponsors the sharing of pertinent information; there's a lot of forward propelling energy when people share a common purpose. You should take advantage of this opportunity to energize the group, set realistic expectations, and set guidelines to complete the project within the approved budget and timeline. Mike Sisco, CEO of MDE Enterprises, makes a compelling argument and gives a comprehensive action plan for a winning kickoff. By following the right steps to prepare, he held a knockout kickoff with attendants from 12 team members from four company departments located in seven separate physical locations! He advises including these steps in your kickoff preparation:

- Develop project goals: Defining these deliverables and goals will aid your decision regarding planning, collecting, and allocating resources for the product. Ask: Why should stakeholders care? Why are you creating this product at this point?

- Identify team members and assign responsibilities — Resources vary based on the product's complexity and size. Be sure to consider what's needed from the design stage, marketing, development, operations, and of course, support.

- Create a rough product plan: Map out the risks and opportunities. This helps confirm whether you have the right resources and helps determine the appropriate timelines for tasks and milestones.

- Define critical success factors: Asking questions here will give you a clearer image of what you need to achieve: Why is the product so valuable to the company? How will you know you've succeeded? What will be the determining factors? Refine and redefine your specific success criteria and confirm these with stakeholders; bring this up when speaking with stakeholders prior to the kickoff. What is the one action that must be taken without any error to make the product awesome? What would exceed your wildest dreams? Assure them that some questions are off the record so you can understand their specific expectations and reservations for the product/service. Holding these stakeholder conversations also help in accumulating a list of high-level functional requirements.

Finally, the Kickoff

Once you are done, it's time to bring together the team. In theory, the kickoff meeting should have an unbridled energy, and teammates should leave the meeting full of ideas and a desire to source solutions. In practice, however, kickoff meetings can be boring or even totally awkward. As a startup or an enterprise, the key to a great kickoff meeting is involving people rather than only reviewing your pre-kickoff documents. Interestingly, Kevin Hoffman, a design consultant at Rosenfeld Media, strongly believes in pursuing a design studio approach to growing creativity. A timeless approach to ideation in industrial design and architecture, this technique is all about building relationships with coworkers and can be executed with groups between 10 to 60 in under a few hours.

Here are some helpful activities for the group to consider:

- Feasibility and priority: Detail and plan your discussed features on a chart based on feasibility and business value. Establish a priority list and stick with it through various development stages.

- Card sorting — Write out discussed functionality, add-ons, and features on index cards, don't go crazy with them, and then have each person go through the deck to categorize highest and lowest priorities; a top-down approach works well here.

- Gut test — Gather screenshots of product images/web pages, then make a carousel presentation in front of the team. Each teammate should be given an opportunity to rank each image with a score range of 1-5; you will be able to sus out everyone's aesthetic leanings.

- Fishbowl conversations — When discussing the pre-kickoff activities or engaging in group activities, arrange your seating in a circular fashion, think of a fishbowl, giving everyone in the group a chance at face-to-face contact and the opportunity to contribute.

It should be obvious that there's no denying that an agenda and/or kickoff document are necessary to keep the activities on track.

Lean & Business Model Canvas

This is a straightforward plan for product and market development, and the Lean Canvas was gotten from the Business Model Canvas. It overlaps nicely with a project kickoff plan in defining the fundamental problems it's solving, customer segments, its peculiar offering, details of the solution, and key metrics. What is the main difference between the Lean Canvas and the Project Kickoff Plan? One is more strategic, while the other is more tactical; they are complementary to each other, but only to some degree.

On the other hand, the Lean Canvas has four fundamental differences from its predecessor, Business Model Canvas. Based on musings by Cloudfire's CEO Ash Maurya, these changes help companies address the riskiest elements of business ideas. By focusing on problems instead of critical partners, you reduce the chance of building the wrong product. By considering key metrics instead of crucial resources, you keep the product focused on impacting only the metrics that matter. It's important not to get overwhelmed by the lean canvases — they aren't meant to be perfect, so at this early stage, it's more important to record stuff down on paper.

If you're a larger company, the Business Model Canvas template might be a more suitable option because it takes existing elements and resources into account. Key partners, essential resources, and customer relationships are left out of the Lean Canvas, but all have a tremendous impact on how enterprises design, manufacture, and distribute products. For instance, the upgraded version of your app might have more functionality and twice as fast, but it may only appeal to your high-paying customers.

For a hybrid option, you can employ the Javelin Experiment Board for converting goals into actionable items. This approach combines the Get out of the building mentality of Lean Canvas with the enterprise elements of the Business Model Canvas.

Concept Maps & Mockups

A super helpful way of defining the tangible and intangible aspects of your product, concept maps begin with the main idea (or concept) and then branch out to highlight how that main idea can be broken down into well-defined topics. Concept mapping is a systemized process that focuses on a particular topic that can involve input from one or more participants. The aim is to produce a visual that shows how ideas and concepts are interrelated. When making a concept map, hold these tips close to your heart:

- Specific language — The less ambiguity you bring to the table, the better and faster understanding will permeate the whole design

- Iterate ruthlessly — Start by drawing the map early in the product definition phase and redraw it repeatedly. With each iteration, you may discover new and interesting relationships between concepts

- Introduce hierarchy — You can make a smaller set of key concepts and propositions stand out, permitting readers to get a sense of the overall structure and dive into detail as required

- Bring in stakeholders — The power of concept maps lies in collaboration, so validate it with stakeholders to ensure your vision is aligned

Hugh Dubberly, CEO of Dubberly Design Office, says that concept maps aid in fostering deeper knowledge by bringing to mind both the forest and trees in a single view. While working on a rehauling of Sun Microsystems' Java landing page, he discovered this approach instrumental to understanding the structure and purpose of its over 110,000 pages. He instantly experienced benefits such as a deeper understanding of technical structures, quality feedback, and additional trust from stakeholders.

As a concurrent process, you can also create concept mockups, which are instant sketches that show the product's overall structure. According to former AOL UX designers Bryce Glass, Richard Fulcher, and Matt Leacock, concept mockups are an excellent foundation for later product documentation. Concept mockups can serve as early sketches for wireframes, explorations for detailed mockups, and provide visuals for storyboards. Similar to concept maps, concept mockups offer a unique space to think differently, generates a variety of ideas quickly, and are a low-risk way of exploring alternatives with stakeholders. Sean Hodge, Editor at Tuts+, highlights in great detail the importance of sketching for product design. In his opinion, sketching out a concept map or mockup is the quickest way of experimenting with various product ideas — and the larger the project, the more ideas will need explaining, and the more important sketching will be. To see how this can be tailored for a complex product on the market, you can look up the conceptual sketch of Apple's iWatch.

Researching Products

The procedure required to define and carry out research on a product is linked since you are unable to effectively define a product unless you know the context in which it exists. As soon as you've defined the product idea and the needed research, which naturally covers user and market research, gives the other half of the foundation for great design.

The user's mind is a competitive and deep space. To further complicate it all, you need to understand your customers as a collective entity and on an individual level. Market research may start by examining demographics while user research seeks out information that challenges and qualifies the segmentation. Both kinds of research have a role in innovation and can discover gaps that propel new product ideas. We'll discuss how market research analyses, user surveys, heuristic evaluations, usability reports, and analytics help you see the large playing field in conjunction with the immediate need.

Why is Research Important?

Simply put, if you have no idea who you're building the product for, then you have no idea why you should be building. And if you don't know the reason, then it matters little how you build. You are well on the fast track to disaster if this is how you currently operate. Louis Rosenfeld, the founder of Rosenfeld Media, says the reason behind product research can be found in the simple fable of the elephant and the blind men. As the story goes, some blind men walk into a bar and encounter an elephant — one feels a trunk and swears it's a snake, another feels a leg and claims it's a tree. Nobody sees the whole picture; you may try by squinting. Just like the blind men, unless you have an ever-evolving research strategy, you'll be hardpressed to show how all the pieces align to make a cohesive whole that informs your product-building decisions.

If you are yet to have a product on the market, research tactics like competitive profiling and market segmentation helps you determine the perfect timing and for your investments. According to Rebecca Bagley, CEO of Nortech, market research helps you separate distinguishable and addressable markets:

- Total addressable market (TAM) — Captures the total revenue opportunity available for your product. Consider this to be your product's jurisdiction.

- Serviceable available market (SAM) — Refers to the section of the addressable market you can realistically compete in without losing sleep. Consider this your product residence.

Market Segmentation Report

TA document that examines potential customers based on their specific needs and characteristics. Broadly speaking, customers are segmented by benefit, psychology, geography, demographics, behaviors, or a combination of the listed factors. Based on Inc Magazine, segmentation reports should cover three main market points — benefits, descriptive, behavioral. All of these benefit bases are made up of customer traits, which you can use to create personas during the Analysis phase. Here I have summarized these three benefit points coupled with company examples:

- Behavioral points — Compared to descriptive bases, these are significantly difficult to measure; these points dig deep into understanding the reasoning behind each purchase. Behavioral bases include deep-seated motivations of buyers such as brand loyalty, personality, lifestyle, and social class.

- Descriptive points — As the name implies, these include factors that describe demographics like family size, gender, age, gender, income, and the likes. It also includes geography options like region, population, and climate. Due to its ease of measurement, this is usually the most commonly used base.

- Benefit points — This segmentation approach is the most logical and assumes demarcations exist in the service of consumer benefits. One misconception in all of this, of course, is that consumers aren't always logical, neither do they know the specific benefit they want. What then is the answer? Well, a combination of benefit points is a closer mirror of real life.

Bert Markgraf, President of North46 Technologies, explains how different prominent companies focus on different segment bases. McDonald's segments by a descriptive base and targets children with Happy Meals while creating its popular breakfast menu for working adults. On the other hand, Patagonia segments by behavioral base using products that emphasize responsible, sustainable, and quality production; factors that carry over regardless of environmental usage. Jes Koepfler and Victor Yocco, both Usability Researchers at Intuitive Company, say that market research and complementary segmentation reports should be used to direct and serve user research. However, due to strict segmentation can let you miss out on potentially profitable secondary customers. The tactic should then be used in tandem with user research so you can see beyond what's recorded on paper.

Survey Data

It is on record that Jobs once said to a group; It *isn't the consumers' job to know what they want.* While that's arguably true because no one wants a committee of customers designing their product, survey results still serve as a standard measuring tool. They certainly aren't compulsory for product success, although any insight into the customer's mind is better than guessing.

David Masters, Editor at Tuts+, opines that online surveys are a low-cost tactic that lets you see data patterns quickly. Interviews and focus groups can provide in-depth research, but they're costly; you need to prepare questions, find potential customers, pay people to interview, and other tedious activities. In the event that you're short on resources, online surveys offer a leaner and scalable way of quickly gathering volumes of information — especially if you don't have a usable prototype yet. Here below are a few tips should you decide to go this route:

- Set clear goals: What do you want to know? Who are you talking to? Short answers are always better, so make sure you only ask questions you need direct answers to. A 3-minute survey will give you concise data than a 20-minute interview.

- Pen to paper: Draft every question you need answers to. Once your list populates to about 10 or 15 questions, rephrase them in different combinations in a way that all focus on the issue at hand.

- Edit like a maniac: Group your original list into common themes and then pick one out of each theme. For maximum punch, you want five questions; cut out anything beyond seven.

- Question draftsmanship: Closed questions have a limited choice of answers. Use them. These may either be binary or multiple choice. Open-ended questions let you find things you never considered and let you learn the language of customers. No matter your choice, the simpler and shorter your questions, the better your responses.

- <u>Line them up</u>: The most important questions go first. If you need more information, then ask them follow up questions. Make sure that you are mindful of what you do in the beginning, as this may count for or against you.

For example, Jonathan Kochis, Partner at Treble Apps, used survey data to help refine the features of a consumer-first mobile project for 3M Canada. If your budget permits, he advises investing in a research firm to refine your questions and locate the perfect set of participants. If you're on a budget, taking the above advice with Fluid Surveys or SurveyMonkey can still get you decent results. Regardless of your approach, he cautions you to be highly selective with open-ended questions because they create friction for respondents and can be tedious to make sense of. Constant Contact has a comprehensive list of survey questions linked to answer choices. To start, you can then use this sample survey template from SurveyMonkey. Surveys are necessary, and they take out the guesswork from the equation, effectively making the process smoother.

Heuristic Evaluations

The moment you develop a working prototype, a detailed heuristic evaluation and user review can be a low-cost method of evaluating your early iterations against best usability practices. Heuristic evaluations are also important for competitive benchmarking since you can compare competitors against the same criteria. Based on Neil Turner, founder of UX For The Masses' statement, heuristic reviews can be carried out by non-UX practitioners so long as they follow a set of guidelines. While heuristic evaluations are cheap and usually only require two days, they don't precisely tell you the usability of a system. This happens because you're not testing with real users, therefore, the data may suffer from subjectiveness and inconsistency; they are, after all, being carried out by different people. That being said, they are still a great reality check since you'll be able to catch glaring UX violations. I have taken the time to summarize a scenario-based approach. Here you go:

- Define your usability review scenarios — Plan out common and pertinent user tasks. Who needs the product, and is this their first time using it? What task are they trying to go through? What exactly is their goal? Here's an example for you; when evaluating a laptop, you would examine processes like sending an email, typing up a document, and watching movies.

- Walk through every scenario: Now that each scenario is defined, you need to go through the steps required to achieve user goals. Can they see how it is done? And how do they know that their action was correct? Walkthrough each scenario until you think the user achieved their goal or gave up.

- Complete a heuristic review scorecard — It's best to have 3-5 people do this. Remember that a high score doesn't equal your product is usable, only that it should be usable. Oracle uses a straightforward 10-point list of heuristics gauging everything from application complexity to frequency and usefulness of error messages. Usability issues are classified as either low, medium, or top-level severity with supporting documentation. The team then segments the top 10 most important issues for immediate fixing. Being curious about what a full heuristic report may look like, look up this heuristic evaluation of Apple iTunes.

User Research Report

Once you've checked your product or prototype is in line with best practices, it's time to verify those findings with authentic users. Tactics like tree testing, card sorting, moderated user testing, unmoderated user testing, and other techniques can all be employed. While usability testing is significantly more expensive than heuristic evaluations because you need to plan and recruit for controlled experiments; and there is no better way to see how your product might perform in the wild. David Sherwin, Design Director at Frog, observes that market research explains what users do and when they do it, but user research provides the picture by answering why they do it and how your product design can react accordingly.

He advises to follow a 5-stage system:

- Objectives: Craft framing questions like, Who would share video clips? Why would they share these clips? Give priority to the most important questions, and then translate them into focused objectives like how frequent TV viewers in Turkey decide what shows to watch now or record for later viewing.

- Hypotheses: Take your framing questions from the previous step, spend up to 8 minutes, on average, sketching answers. You may generate attitudinal hypotheses, behavioral hypotheses, or feature-related hypotheses.

- Methods — Categorize all your hypotheses based on themes and then assign testing tactics. Here is an instance, observational and contextual interviews are superb for laying a foundation of knowledge. Paper prototyping, diary studies, card sorting, and other collaborative activities help explore designs.

- Conduct: Bring on board eight users for three testing sessions each. Create an interview guide and then document it all, from photos, notes, and right down to videos. Continuously ask yourself if you're unearthing what you need to learn in order to hit your objectives. If not, change your approach.

- Synthesize: The why holding up the data is more important than the what. Are there patterns that suggest you need new trends? Did what you learn affect how you should craft your research objective? Also, do you need to change the design activities that you've outlined?

As you probably must have guessed, if not totally been convinced, there are many different approaches you can build into your testing design. Bryan McClain and Demetrius Madrigal, founders of Metric Lab, provide a helpful list of Dos and Don'ts for usability testing. For instance, you should get involved and observe as much testing as possible, but don't jump to design conclusions based on only a few tests. And while you shouldn't hide from participants using a one-way mirror, discard the temptation to turn your testing session into a product demo.

By following a rigorous user testing plan, Volusion was actually able to shoot paid conversions by 10% and product trials by 6%. They implemented a very specific formula of video-recorded testing sessions and A/B testing; it's certainly proof that the process works.

If you're shopping for a leaner user research approach, you can follow this user testing framework, which is quick and dirty; you would be done in less time than it takes to eat lunch and then document your plan in a simple format that resonates with stakeholders.

Analytics Reports

These are simply quantitative complements to the mostly qualitative processes we've discussed so far. Qualitative methods like heuristic reviews and user research are bottom-up methods of analyzing users, while analytics are top-down since you're breaking down broad data into concise insights. According to Jennifer Cardello, Director at the Nielsen Norman Group, analytics has traditionally informed marketing strategy but is seeing growing usage in design and user research. Because qualitative research is obviously expensive, you can first get a bird's-eye view of potential issues and testing scenarios based on analytics reports.

In the case of user research, the analytics data serve three important functions for highlighting tests and validating already existing ones:

- Pointing to issues: Weekly metric reports can highlight issues in web-based products. For instance, you may find out that conversions suddenly dipped after a site redesign.

- Investigating issues: If any issues come up, you can take up an investigation. Is the dip in conversions coming from a specific device? Yes? Then you could design a device-specific A/B user test to check for solutions.

- Qualitative research: Analytics can also pinpoint hold-up spots that arise during user testing. For instance, study participants don't know where to get information because a word on the site is unclear. With an amazing tool like Google Analytics, you can then look up the keyword traffic for that term. Discovering that there's a high volume verifies that the problem is worth your time. If you're interested in particular user segments, you can also employ cohort analysis to determine what further research and testing are needed. For instance, you can treat Black Friday shoppers as a cohort, scrutinize their behavior, and design user tests accordingly.

In case you don't have a working product, analytics are still vital for doing market research. According to Inc Magazine, backlinking and keyword analysis are equally effective yet lean methods. Taking on a tool like Google Adwords, you can check for search volumes and discover consumer interest as well as competitors. Analyzing backlinks will also tell you whether competitors are promoting similar products.

Research, Test, Validate

Market research allows you to see the broad context, while user research aids you learn things that are immediately practical. Whether you have an existing product or hanging on the cusp of your Eureka! moment, both will play an important part in your product development. When you integrate market research with user research, you have a way to listen to the market as well as individual users. With that knowledge in mind, you can move forward and design solutions then test them to see if they actually work. Your raw research will be especially useful as it starts to take shape and form during the Analysis phase.

Analyzing Users

A great product experience begins with a good understanding of your users. Not only do you want to find out who they are, but you should also want to dive deeper into their psyche, motivations, fears, and mentality. But how do we accurately what our users really want? User analysis and modeling, and analysis will be the ultimate reality check on whether people would actually be excited about your product. As soon as you get a rough idea of your product definition and how it snugly fits the current market, it's time to dive into user-centric modeling. Your aim here is to simply understand their struggles, know the details of the circumstance, put them in context, and gauge their reactions to your offering.

We will consider personas & scenarios, user matrices, requirements documents, and experience maps. You will learn to make your product respond smoothly to customer problems. In the end, this will help you iterate to solve problems you might never have even considered.

Why Analysis is Important

User analysis answers questions about end-users tasks and goals so that these findings can help make decisions about development and eventual design. Specifically, you'll be able to highlight roles and define leanings that aren't always possible through market research, such as knowledge, comfort with similar products, use cases & environments, and usage frequency. These insights ensure that feature changes are drawn from data gained from users who will pay side-by-side with the opinions of stakeholders.

Smashing Magazine thinks user-centered analysis helps get more profitable products to market at a quicker pace. Because user analysis allows customers to decide the path of your product, the insights you gain can help circumvent time-crunching decision-making processes and politics. When you hit a wall due to conflicting views, user analysis lets you propel in the right direction based on inarguable facts. We've summarized some specific benefits below:

- Better products: Processes that involve end-users as well as understand business objectives will always end in products that work better for their intended design.

- Cheaper to fix problems: User analysis helps you line up your product with reality to make changes while it's still mostly an idea recorded on scrap paper. A wireframe or prototype is way cheaper than a technical fix to a live product.

- Ease of use is a basic requirement: Customers often use the terms usability and user experience when describing qualities they need in products. Therefore, user analysis pushes your product to have better selling points.

Personas

At first glance, it may appear difficult to build a person out of thin air, creating a persona is a crucial first step to understanding the psyche of potential customers. Personas help to keep focus product decisions by adding a layer of real-world attributes to the conversation. They are almost like another person in the room when making important product decisions. However, personas shouldn't address all needs of your product or represent all audiences but should rather focus on the key needs of the most significant user groups. Remember that trying to please everyone with your product is one of the quickest ways to fall short of your goals. According to Content Crafter at Buffer's Kevan Lee, personas teach you to internalize potential customers so you can actually relate to them as carbon-based, real-life humans. He advises using three to five personas since this number is large enough to cover a large sample of customers yet small enough to be specific. Below, I have summarized the information you'll want to capture:

- Give the persona a name: You can decide on whatever name you like, but make it believable; this way, the person feels its tangibility. The name can also be labeled using segmentation, for instance, Smith the Optimist.

- Identify the role: Surveys can be very helpful when capturing this data. For instance, Buffer's survey showed a large percentage of users are small/medium business owners. They went on to use this information to make an " SMB" persona for this purpose.

- Include vivid information: While gender, age, device type, and usage are important, you also want to understand psychology. What are their strongest fears and highest aspirations? You can make use of metrics tools for demographics and educated guesses for psychographics. Alan Klement, a former Product Designer at Interactive Pioneers, says that basic personas sometimes lack the causalities that direct to consumer purchases. In his opinion, interviews and a focus on psychology are required to flesh out personas into characters that can be studied with regards to their anxieties, motivations, and touchpoints during the buying process. As you start fleshing out your personas, you can keep them better rooted in reality by conducting segmented interviews. You'll be able to add copious amounts of real-world data into your personas by interviewing existing customers, referrals, and prospects. To keep it casual, you can use a persona template or other robust solutions that let you attach personas to prototypes.

Defining Your Vision

While use cases consider how your personas might use the product, the experience map takes a much higher-level view of the user as part of a hero's journey, helping you better shape your product to be the ultimate sidekick. Brandon Schauer, CEO of Adaptive Path, opines that experience mapping unlocks the key customer moments that can be optimized for a more high-end overall experience. If done well, an experience map presents the entire customer experience, highlighting the highs and lows people feel when interacting with your service/business. Here are the four steps to making the most of your experience map:

- Uncover the truth — Search your company for qualitative and quantitative data on the experiences you want to map. Look at a range of data sources such as interviews, customer surveys, web analytics, and call logs. In order to discover and fill out knowledge gaps, data triangulation is advised.

- Plot your course: Experience maps should contain the lens—a persona through which the journey can be viewed—the journey model, and takeaways; insights gleaned from the process and design principles gained through the journey.

- Relate the story: Your map should have a start point, middle, and an ending. Highlight what insights are crucial to the narrative and what are simply space fillers. Like a good poster, your map requires hierarchy; what stands out immediately compared to what may get cut out

- Circulate the map: Present it at meetings, post it on the wall, print it in a tabloid size so executives can see it. Ensure all stakeholders can use your map as a tool to peruse the world as customers do. In each step of the mapping process, ensure you point back to the customer's actions, hurdles, motivations, and questions. What action is the customer taking at each stage of the map? Why should they move to the next stage? What uncertainties might hinder their forward progression? And what implementation, cost, or other obstacles stand in their way?

Chris Ridson, Design Director at Adaptive Path, observes that the inputs of an experience map can be broken out into two parts. User discovery catalogs touchpoints while user research considers customer feelings, thoughts, and actions. Combining both lets, you see themes of how different touchpoints at different times are experienced — thereby unearthing expectations gaps, pain-points, and acres of opportunity. Following the above process will open your eyes to see beyond logical wants. Joyce Hostyn, the former Director of Customer Experience at OpenText, holds that experience maps can help brands completely reinvent consumer wishes. For instance, by mapping out that most buyers experience uncertainty between the time of order and delivery, Domino's was able to cover that gap and create a *Domino's Tracker* app that tracks pizza delivery in real-time. While experience mapping can be extremely subjective and will differ based on the company, you can use try out templates as an experiment.

User Task Matrix

While user stories examine and scrutinize how your product is used and experience maps show a beginning and end image, a user task matrix looks at the frequency of use. In the instance above, the task matrix describes the various methods (and their frequencies based on persona) for attaining the goal of booking an airline ticket. The user task matrix lends you a helping hand to identify the non-negotiable aspects of the user experience. For instance, our above matrix shows that the most important task is searching travel routes since it's used multiple times by all three personas. You can use this to guide design decisions by ensuring the search route function is part of the basic navigation instead of a discoverable element. Stephanie Troeth, UX Consultant at MailChimp, subscribes to a more collaborative approach to user task matrices; her matrix approach provides a broader snapshot of personas and the experience map by sifting through the lens of contexts for motivations and perceptions.

In comparison to the traditional user matrix, her version is more visual and thus lets you see patterns quickly and prioritize accordingly. For her social running app, the above matrix quickly displayed that locals would likely be most engaged in the app, and therefore the feature set, communications, and marketing needed to appeal to that user group first. Stephanie's user matrix is unsurprisingly complementary because her version aids in the provision of a high-level view that you can feed into the classical user matrix. As was already highlighted, the user matrix can be important in identifying particular audiences, pinpointing vital features, and validating value propositions.

User Content Matrix

If your product is software or cloud-based, a matrix will help you better grasp how your current content satisfies user needs, where you can significantly improve, and how to prioritize content improvements. Unsurprisingly, Colleen Jones, Founder of Content Science, believes that a content matrix will aid you in eliminating any content that is redundant and outdated. Considering that most stakeholders prefer context to details, a matrix makes available flexibility in letting you show only the columns and rows necessary to make your point. Creating a content matrix can provide four specific benefits:

- An acute awareness of priorities — Understanding what content is present in your product (and why) helps flesh out questions about usefulness that otherwise may not come up.

- Operational constraints — When you fill out the matrix, you may find new constraints to solutions. Here's an example, users may need a continuously updated home screen on your app, but you may realize that you lack the technical resources to make this happen. A content matrix brings up evaluations that may help you discover second-best options so you don't move forward under false assumptions.

- A common theme: Your users more than likely don't talk like you do. A content matrix assists you to maintain consistency in tone and terminology, effectively limiting your chances of going overboard on language-specific verbiage.

- Scale: The better your understanding of the scale of content for your product, the better you can design the product. A matrix lets you see if you need to think about 100 or 1000 pages worth of content, which aids in creating the perfect number of design iterations.

Prioritized Requirements Spreadsheet

At this point, you will have done sufficient user analysis to have an idea of important features. After all, you should know by now that your product requirements should be derived from user requirements. While it isn't necessary to go into specific detail as the product requirements document and features specifications document made in the Implementation phase, you should be able to separate nice-to-haves from must-haves. A word from Jeff Sauro, the Founder of Measuring Usability: there exist multiple prioritization techniques for cutting down on impossibly long feature lists. A percentage of the techniques require more user testing, while others do not:

- Kano Modeling — Ask a section of your users to rate how much they enjoy certain features when they are shipped in the product and also how much they will miss those features if they're removed. Doing this will find you the sweet spot that is the satisfaction gap, a belt that clearly shows you a side-by-side view of must-have and nice-to-have features in your app or system.

- Top Task Analysis: Give qualified users a randomized list of straightforward tasks, then ask them to pick their top five. Quickly and without stress, you will start to identify the tasks most important to users.

- Pareto Analysis — Also goes by the name the 80/20 rule, which is a method that can quickly isolate must-have features from nice-to-haves. Sort your features from highest to lowest; using most votes in a top-task, most revenue, add up the total, then calculate the percentage for each item. Your most important features are the ones that score highest.

- Quality Function Deployment: Begin with a prioritized list of features gleaned from top-task analysis, then combine this with a list of functions. A QFD ranks the features that best meet user needs.

- Gap Analysis: Give some customers your first iteration of prioritized features and ask them to rate them in order of satisfaction and importance. Then, use the formula: Importance + (Importance - Satisfaction) to expose an opportunity for improvement.

- Cause & Effect: Because UX issues can be complex, this analysis can unearth multiple causes for each problem, further giving you the ability needed to troubleshoot as deep as you like. Make a set of cause-and-effect diagrams by asking users questions. Why questions are the best type of questions in this case. The point is to uncover the root causes by following actual symptoms or simulated scenarios.

- Failure Mode Effect Analysis: This helps you understand the adverse effects of some actions. It can point out cases in which you can upgrade the product more by remedying what's broken than by piling on more features. An FMEA produces a Risk Priority Number based on the severity, difficulty, and commonality of issues.

If you are shopping for a leaner approach, then Ian McAllister, General Manager at Amazon, has a word for you. He believes a theme-based method is an effective yet lightweight approach. He makes a list of themes for each product; user acquisition, user retention, then assign projects to each theme. Only after this does he prioritize projects based on cost versus benefits. It's fairly simple, so you would only need a forced ranking spreadsheet to get started.

Do You Know Your User?

If your product isn't created for users, then logic dictates that you only built it to satisfy you. Your users aren't concerned by the fact that your app can do a thousand things and then some more. The million-dollar question on their mind is, will it work for them? Are any of these features going to satisfy their needs/wants? When it comes to going deep into the psyche of your user, casually saying that they are *16 to 43-year-old marketers who need an app to simplify inbox sorting* doesn't even begin to help. As you have already seen, you need to get to acquaint yourself with your user; know them as individuals, understand how and why they'd use your app. Get into how often they might use it, then all the experiences that may hinder them from truly having a wonderful time with the app. That multi-dimensional understanding is the only way you'll be able to prioritize your features appropriately — otherwise, you might

4

The Design Process

From Hootsuite, Twitter to apps like Dropbox for iOS, every product first lives on paper or directly on the screen before they come burst to life. The design stage is a rite of passage for every well-made product — they're either desirable, or they just don't make the cut. The definition of design should be simple and without fluff, but today's world demands a vortex list of considerations in order to produce a functional product. Did it help? Easy to use? Does it feel a bit familiar after your first encounter? Designers have a solemn responsibility since customers have problems, and the product needs to give them a sense of ease and well-being. The product is simply a vehicle for conveying an incredible experience.

Although it might feel like the process is filled with crumpled paper and, maybe, a broken screen or more, you can rest assured knowing there is a method to the madness. I will explain the different forms of documentation you can use as your idea grows into a design that's guided by user research. Continue to read to learn about wireframing and conceptual sketching, low and high fidelity prototypes, and the intricacies that accompany design specification.

Iterated Sketching & Wire-framing

Sketches are arguably the most prevalent documentation you'll create as you go about designing. Usually, the general workflow is mockup sketching followed by usability testing followed by a lot of iteration. Regardless of the tool you use to differ to for your sketches, it's crucial to keep user personas at the fore of your thoughts. As you create your drawings, always reference the personas you built during the Analysis phase, so you never lose sight of your users. Below, I will explain a bit about rough sketching and wireframing.

1. Rough Sketching

It is possible to create rough sketches with anything that makes pigments on a surface. Crayons, pencils, markers, pens, Paper App, and even the simplistic yet useful, Microsoft Paint. Laura Busche, a design writer at Smashing Magazine, says that sketching by hand has distinct benefits for aiding concentration, flexibility improvement, and extending memory. Drawing by hand is one of the fastest ways to visualize a concept, so it should always serve as your backup method. Product design firm ZURB leans heavily on paper sketching to present the function and app navigation. They prefer sharpies to other tools because they limit the amount of detail and focus the sketch on just the broad points. Paper sketching is all about communicating for the company, whether it be interaction or flow, without getting buckled down by unnecessary information. ZURB isn't thinking feedback on the iconography, copy, or design; all they are focused on in this stage is communicating what exists in the realm of thought. Yes, paper sketching is fast, focused, and flexible, but it's unfortunately limited and unscalable; the interaction is also limited as there is no way to link sketches the way you do in digital spaces.

2. Wireframing

Digital wireframing software abounds, but there are really only a few serious apps worth checking out, such as Axure and Balsamiq. If you plan on going the paper route, you could also just make your rough sketch a wireframe by breaking it up into sections of the page and adding grid lines and boxes where appropriate. Wireframing should function as the backbone of the product.

According to the CEO of HeadScape, Paul Boag, wireframing saves money and time, which are resources you should not take for granted. It also provides benefits like early testing and doing away with the fear of change that comes from finalizing ideas/design. The minute you have a low fidelity wireframe in the bag, you can immediately test it with users. Going this route allows you to collect feedback on features users lean towards, label, and choosing the right visual hierarchy for your design. And it is didn't spend considerable effort, it's no big deal to change up your plan. UX Movement's Editor-in-Chief, Anthony Tseng, says you can also use high fidelity if your goal is to show the actual form and function better to get stakeholders on your side. Although they may take more time and are less ideal for quick feedback, high fidelity wireframes give explicit representations of the interface and leave no questions in stakeholders and users' minds.

Detailed Mockups

It goes without saying that it will depend on your process and what you want to achieve; detailed mockups can either be the highest-level fidelity wireframes or the next iteration of concept mockups. There are companies that will skip wireframing altogether and jump straight to create a lower fidelity concept mockup before upgrading fidelity to a detailed mockup. Other companies may follow a more evolutionary path that uses wireframes as the skeletons for mockups. You might hear both terminologies – *wireframing* and *mockups* – used as one and the same; they are two different types of documents. The wireframes layout the structure, and then texture and fidelity are injected to turn it into a mockup, which doubles as a model of the system/app.

Based on opinions shared by UXPin's CEO, Marcin Treder, a detailed mockup is usually a design draft or function as the actual visual design. It is an almost photorealistic and well-made detailed mockup that encourages people actually to review the visual side of the project. On the one hand, wireframes might contain lines, shapes, and elements with a bit more detail, when shooting for high fidelity. On the other hand, a detailed mockup always shows color choices, specific fonts and presents what the final look will be. Nick Pettit, a designer at Treehouse, reaffirms that detailed mockups are helpful as a means of communicating design but shouldn't be treated as a bridge into development territory. He goes further to say that the process of spending hours creating a detailed mockup as a spec sheet for designers is no longer useful due to the rise of Agile methods and responsive design. Also, lower fidelity wireframes can be easier to iterate since they require less effort, while prototyping can be a much simpler way to bridge the functional gap.

Prototypes

If wireframes are made up of structure, then prototypes are concerned with experience. Wireframes or mockups can be integrated and made to work seamlessly, as seen in apps like Invision; this helps to produce a clickable prototype. As seen above, there are multiple levels for workflow and fidelity. Josh Porter, the former Director of UX at HubSpot, has complete faith in a leaner workflow where you move straight from sketching to prototyping. In his opinion, sketches require less time but can answer the same functional questions like, What elements go on the page, and what can we do to them?

While more effort can be given to building out a prototype, this in no way implies that wireframes and mockups are dead, it merely means that more time can be reallocated from developing static assets towards interactive assets. The true power of prototyping is its ability to get teams to think less about deliverables and more about practicality. There are some successful companies that have gone on to release prototypes as their first product! It's all about working with elements that suit your situation and, of course, understanding the market.

In this bit, we'll discuss both low and high fidelity prototypes and their different use cases. I find that knowing both and getting a feel for what they may be used for helps immensely with design and choice:

1. Low Fidelity Prototypes

When people talk about rapid-fire prototyping and Lean UX, they're usually referring to low fidelity prototypes. Low fidelity prototypes are invaluable for avoiding tunnel vision by focusing on the refinement of interaction rather than the details of visual and technical implementation. They can be built using online apps (Balsamiq, or Invision, to mention a few) or coded in HTML the old fashioned way. Entrepreneur and speaker Andrew Chen believes that low-fidelity prototyping is one of the best ways to incorporate user-driven design. Because you need your product to be the perfect one, low fidelity prototypes built in an online app may be visually unappealing but can help you iterate faster as opposed to using a coded prototype. He's described four particular benefits, which are presented here:

- Honest feedback — People tend to focus on the visuals of a detailed, perfect prototype instead of its value proposition. They may also feel reluctant to build on your idea since it is beyond their capability to replicate.

- Geared for A/B testing — A/B testing thrives off variety at the UI layer, where small changes can be tested and optimized. Therefore, 10-20 rough iterations in UI can give more insights than pixel-perfect ones.

- Embrace mistakes — Pivoting with a low-fidelity prototype is easier since fewer resources are involved, and the team isn't as defensive about changing.

- Focuses on flow rather than pages — One of the key decisions isn't the look of a page, but what happens before and after. Low fidelity prototypes allow you to draw and link up lots of small pages, play with interaction, and carry out other activities when the environment is more sandbox-like.

Here's a rule of thumb that has never failed: If you are going the route of low fidelity, a rule of thumb is to keep attention on 20% of the features that will be interacted with 80% of the time.

2. High Fidelity Prototypes

These prototypes are more useful when you are at the last legs of design and considering factors like branding, look and feel, and other crucial details. The high fidelity prototype gives you the ability to get as close as possible to the real product at a lower cost. Similar to low fidelity prototypes, you can also use online apps to create a high fidelity version. In the opinion of Marty Cagan, Partner at the Silicon Valley Product Group, high fidelity prototypes can push for a deeper level of collaboration between product managers, designers, and engineers to expose what's needed for a viable product. Higher fidelity prototypes offer benefits like:

- An early image of the product — Sales, marketing, and business development can seamlessly come together to provide an understanding of the product early enough, so preparations are well on the way.

- Reduced development time — Confirming a high-fidelity prototype with users may drastically drop development since the product is considerably polished, and you may have resolved many of the questions early that otherwise complicate development.

- A better idea of scope: High fidelity prototypes provide more precise information for accurate engineering cost estimates early in the process; this is when they are most useful. This is especially important if your product introduces new technology.

Fidelity aside, Smashing Magazine author Lyndon Cerjeo suggests that prototypes should be built piece by piece, like a puzzle, rather than in one fell swoop. As highlighted by Andrew Chen, an effective method is to start prototyping broadly and widely and then to dive deep into selected areas of the solution with higher fidelity. For instance, the first iteration of a website prototype would build out the critical landing pages, while extended iterations could be higher fidelity and consider intricate details on specific website sections.

Design Specifications

On the one hand, prototypes show interaction and aesthetics, while design specifications detail the processes and artistic elements/assets needed to make all that work. Design specifications are mostly made up of user flow & task flow images, which highlight the functionality and asset & style requirements, which detail the creative and technical details of the visual identity.

User Flow Diagram

User flows, also known as journeys, map the entire realm of circumstances and decisions that influences how someone achieves their goal. This is an exhaustive list and includes the moment the idea forms in the user's head until the goal is attained.

A user flow diagram maps out broad targets such as planning travel or hiring an employee. For instance, two people seeking to purchase movies online may have vastly different experiences. One might enter Amazon.com using the address bar, search for a catalog with intent to buy, and add to the basket, while another might search on Google, click the first result, scour reviews online, compare reviews, and dive deeper into detail before getting into the buying funnel. Therefore, your user flow diagram could become the opposite of lean. According to Wireframes Magazine, the Speech Bubble User Flow above is a practical approach to focusing on the expressed needs and desires of real people as you create the product interaction. As projects gain momentum, it can be easy to get lost in the technical side of things. The Speech Bubble User Flow ensures that focus isn't taken away from the personas you developed in the Analysis stage; it keeps attention locked on where it should be.

Task Flow Diagram

If user flows are holistic by design, then task flows are microscopic in execution. Task flows describe a specific and repeatable series of actions such as setting the time on an alarm clock app. As you see in the above example, task flowcharts are less visually appealing than user flows since they describe almost algorithmic processes. But they are needed in helping you streamline the steps that must be taken to accomplish everything your product promises. Larry Marine, the founder of the Intuitive Design Group, believes that task flow analysis is a crucial UX step that many people skip. Unlike use case analysis, which examines how people interact with systems, task flow analysis examines the details of how people accomplish specific tasks. It's a subtle but essential distinction. Here's an instance, Larry went to a brick-and-mortar shop to observe the steps people took in completing the task of purchasing flowers before applying what he learned towards modifying the task flow of an online florist site. By concerning himself with functions rather than use cases, he became empowered to think outside the product box and see how people could potentially solve a problem rather than how they currently go about it.

Assets & Style Requirements

A product style guide is often called to serve as an outline for the technical and aesthetic specifications of the look and feel. Product style guides will include anything from brand rules describing what emotional states to achieve to technical specifications like file formats, specific pixels, and dimensions of design assets. These guidelines may be brief and loose to promote creativity like Mozilla's brand toolkit or precise and exhaustive.

Brad Haynes, a Product Designer at Salesforce, built the Salesforce style guide around the product rather than a concept. Faced with repetitive questions from his team, he was able to create uniformity in Salesforce's look and feel by rethinking and approaching it as a mobile app. The core of the recent product style guide included the following elements:

- Typography — The design was made simple by restricting it to only one font and listing specific font weights

- Colors — A small segment of the color palette was shown to give just enough information without overwhelming the team.

- Principles — Guidelines linked to simplicity, hierarchy, and alignment were clearly laid out to explain the reasoning behind the product design.

- Iconography — The complete system and library of icons and their technical descriptions were made available

At Yelp, the style guide is stretched and treated as a living document that is of immense benefit to designers and developers, as well. Their style guide inculcates snippets of code to help reduce technical debt. As a result, the integration between their design and development team actually helped reduce the time needed to create new features since the teams could work off of reusable code and updated design pattern libraries.

At this point, you must have realized that the design phase consists of multiple stages and tactics that feed into each other – **Define Design**

Refine – to give life to your idea that translates into an incredible user experience. It matters little if you go low fidelity or high fidelity; the ultimate goal of sketching, wireframing, and prototyping is to deliver great product concepts — not deliverables. If you have drawn something on scrap paper that resembles a solution you can follow-through on, then it goes without saying that there's no tangible value in recreating it in wireframe for the sake of prettiness. Skip that stage altogether. Remember that these things aren't rules so much as they are guides that help; breaking them is still in the cards. And while the design specifications might come off as extra paperwork, an extra ounce of sweat in the design phase can save you a lot of grief during development by being strategic about the reason behind your documentation. Don't create deliverables for the sake of it unless you have nothing better to do, but I know that you have much better things to do, especially as you approach the next phase of implementation.

5

UX Design:
Lean UX vs Agile UX

In the field of UX, acronyms, systems, and methods reign supreme. Buzz words meander at every corner and stop imaginable, from strategic UX, CX, guerrilla research to IA, lean, and everything else in between. Keeping up with everything and making contextual sense of it can be all so tedious. I cannot even lie about that, even if I tried. There is also the issue of new words being invented that do not serve any new function; it's a common case of fancy rebranding using cool terms. Two of these terms that have drawn attention and argument from every quarter are Lean UX and Agile UX. Some argue about the usefulness or lack thereof of being laden with terms that don't differ from already established and accepted tags. The goal of this chapter isn't to make an argument for either, although both will be presented to you. The aim here is to bring to your mind both approaches; history, advantage, application, and hopefully, you will decide for yourself which way to go. Of course, dynamism and methodology should be considered when examining both approaches, and the nature of your service, business, or brand will determine which branch you swing towards.

Agile UX

Agile traces back to software development methodologies created in the 1960s. In the decades that followed, the strategies continued to evolve. By 2001, The Agile Manifesto 5 had introduced a cohesive concept of Agile based on lofty and inspiring goals: working software over documentation, flexible schedules over a rigid timeline, and collaboration over antagonism.6 Sounds pretty great, doesn't it? The Agile process and its varieties, such as Scrum and Kanban, have become the norm in large-scale development efforts. The quick path to functioning software does much to curb the apprehensions of today's executives. Development tasks lend themselves to Agile. Coding is a complex and artful task; however, the code either works or it does not. If it meets performance goals, then, by most accounts, the code is viable. Using Agile, you can build, test, and deploy almost anything, as long as it fits within a sprint. A sprint is any timeboxed interval, though most are a few weeks in length. You determine the work. You complete it. You test it. You deploy it. You move on to the next sprint. After several sprints, you arrive at a fully functioning product. This model works so well for some organizations that Agile has extended into Agile product development, Agile marketing, and—what we will focus on next—Agile UX. In several environments, Agile UX may be a perfect solution. We split a set of tasks into sprints and quickly see results. Our UX and development deliverables align.

Everyone uses a common vernacular. The team digs 10 feet into the mountain, looks around, high-fives, and plans the next 10-foot increment. Tunnels get built. But this immediacy is also where cracks begin to form within an Agile project. Although speed may be a virtue, it misses the small issues that, if left unaddressed, may grow into tremors, crumble the support for your project, and bury you alive. We make trade-offs. Rather than wait for a research study, we interview only a handful of stakeholders. Rather than wait to build wireframes, we advance to a prototype. Rather than wait for conclusive testing results, we repair as we receive feedback. We trade clarity for speed and contemplation for immediacy. These tradeoffs can be compelling, but they are also why Agile UX projects sometimes fail. Why would an Agile UX project fail? After all, many UX research and design processes can be grouped into tasks, and these tasks are frequently iterative. Furthermore, UX deliverables are notoriously document-heavy, and Agile UX promises to lighten this load. People would rather play with a functioning prototype than trudge through detailed documentation. And lastly, people want software now, not months from now. It is hard to argue against any of those points.

But I will. Problems arise from the UX tasks themselves: several are linear and build upon one another. Experienced team members may appreciate the first stages of user experience design, but these early activities are intangible to novices. Research may appear too slow. Personas may appear too silly. Flowcharts may appear too abstract. Wireframes may appear too fastidious. The early steps of a UX process may appear to be sedentary: people talk about building a tunnel, but nobody is digging.

We must realize that digging a tunnel into a mountain and digging a tunnel into a volcano may look very much the same at first. We do not notice the difference until we have reached the middle. Some projects combust without effective planning and research. Planning and research reveal their worth over time. Conversely, we recognize their absence when it is already too late, after having squandered vital weeks on a flawed prototype. We find ourselves running, screaming, and searching for a project's exit. With scorched eyebrows and charred egos, we promise to find a better way next time.

Lean UX

Lean UX is an evolution – a sound merger of business and product development. It finds the halfway point between Waterfall and Agile. An excellent book on Lean UX is Jeff Gothelf and Josh Seiden's Lean UX: Applying Lean Principles to Improve User Experience. The book contains a wealth of helpful tips on everything from team dynamics to prototyping. At the core of Lean UX is the "minimum viable product"—an MVP. To explain this concept, let's return to our example of digging a tunnel through a mountain. A tunnel is a big project. It requires considerable time and resources. Your team needs an assortment of picks, shovels, and perhaps a few sticks of dynamite. All these resources cost money. We chisel, excavate, and detonate. All these activities take time. With every project, we risk wasting time and resources. We chart the wrong course. We run into impenetrable obstacles. We dig into the wrong mountain. The brilliance of Lean UX is its lack of ambition. If Lean UX had a rallying cry, it would be "Let's… not!" In essence, the minimum viable product is the shortest path to success. We reduce risk by avoiding large expenses of time and resources. It is akin to digging the shortest route through the mountain. The route we take is not necessarily ideal, but by completing even this short path, we gain new knowledge. Along the way, we learn about potential pitfalls and uncover veins of gold. But our greatest learning comes from reaching the other side of the mountain. For the first time, we see what awaits us. We may learn that the resulting landscape is not worth the effort—best to stop now. We may learn that an ideal destination is nearly in reach—best to keep on digging. You will find Lean UX practices within small startups and large corporations. An MVP serves as a proof of concept. More than a prototype, it demonstrates the crucial features of a product—not all, just the ones that make the product viable. For example, a map app should display maps. An auction site should accept bids.

A banking kiosk should provide account balances. Once we achieve the minimal viable product, everything else becomes elective. To determine what is crucial and what is elective challenges even the most experienced of teams. What should be included? Whereas an application's stability may be viewed as crucial, an application's aesthetics may not. Does an app require an optimum user experience? I think so, but you may feel differently.

A Lean UX project includes only the necessary. It is practical. It is realistic. And, it is often rather boring. An MVP rarely stirs the heart—it is the minimum, after all. Much of what compels users are the product's details: the micro-interactions, the small gestures, and the tailored experiences. Although the minimum gets the product out your door, it does not necessarily get it into a customer's. An MVP provides us with a start: a glimpse of the other side of the mountain. We can either abandon our effort or keep on digging. Our goal is to reach an ideal state—a product that offers not only the minimum but also all the electives that make an experience optimal and enjoyable. The key to reaching this promised land is buried somewhere deep within your project. You only need to look. Start with an MVP. Add, edit, and delete until the experience is so ideal, so perfect, that no other path through the mountain would be as gratifying.

At the core of Lean UX, you'll find a core set of principles; these principles codify process, collaboration, management. Teams shepherded by all these principles will gain the most out of the Lean UX approach. Begin with these principles to get your teams pointed in the right direction, and bear them in mind as you begin to inculcate the Lean UX methods I will describe soon. You will inevitably have to tailor the Lean UX processes to fit into your business, and the principles highlighted in this chapter will serve as an invaluable aid to you for that work. Essentially, if you're able to implement these principles, you'll find that your organization's culture will take a drastic turn. Of course, some will have a significant impact than others and will be more difficult to integrate completely; others will be easier to act on. Regardless, each principle detailed here will help you build a product design organization that is more collaborative, more cross-functional and a more useful fit for today's reality.

Design thinking is crucial for Lean UX because it takes the explicit position that every part of a business can be handled with design approaches. It provides designers permission and precedent to work beyond their typical boundaries. It also encourages non-designers to use design methods to solve the issues they face in their various roles. Design thinking is an essential foundation that encourages teams to collaborate across positions and consider product design from a holistic perspective.

Another important foundation of Lean UX is *Agile software development*. Developers have been implementing Agile methods for years to cut down their cycle times and provide customer value in a continuous manner. Although Agile approaches can pose process challenges for designers, the core values of Agile are at the heart of Lean UX.

Interestingly, Lean UX uses the four core principles of Agile development to product design:

1. Interactions and individuals over processes and tools. To produce the best solutions quickly, you must involve the entire team. Ideas must be circulated frequently and free. The constraints of prevailing processes and production tools are done away with in favor of interaction with team members.

2. Working software over comprehensive documentation. Every business problem has, arguably, an endless number of solutions, and each team member will have an opinion on which is best. The challenge lies in knowing which solution is best for the business. By building a working software sooner than later, solutions can be assessed for market fit and viability in record time.

3. Customer collaboration over contract negotiation: Teammates collaboration with customers builds a shared understanding of the problem space and proposed solutions. It creates consensus behind decisions. The result? Time-sensitive iterations, real involvement in product making, and team investment in actual learning. It also cuts down dependency on heavy documentation, as everyone on the team is a partic-

ipant in the decision-making process that was used to require written communication and defense.

4. Responding to change: An interesting assumption in Lean UX is that the initial product designs will not be 100%, so the goal should be to figure out what's wrong with them without wasting valuable time. Once we discover what's working and what's not, we adjust our proposals and test again. This input from the market keeps us agile, constantly nudging us in a "more right" direction.

Much of UX design and research is about planning what to do—what will be experienced by users. UX design and research is the precursor to visual design and development, and deciding between Agile or Lean is totally dependent on your project and what you wish to accomplish. In the end, build a process that suits your particular circumstance; a good process provides a wall of protection as well as sponsors action.

6

Visual Design Principles

The grasp of visual weight is reasonably intuitive to most people. Some things are perceived as heavier than others in a layout. They pull your attention without stress. The idea and power to control the user is valuable to a UX designer. Your job, therefore, is to aid users to notice the things that matter. And it is also important not to distract the users from their goals. By introducing visual weight to specific parts of your design, you significantly increase the chance of a user to see them, and you change where their eyes follow next. Remember: visual weight is all so relative. All visual principles are concerned with comparing a design element to whatever is in its vicinity. At its core, there are five visual design principles in the field of UX. There are, of course, subsets that seem to crowd space(see what I did there?), but it all boils down to one principle, an integration of more or just a matter of interpretation and coinage – remember that the field is drowning in terminologies.

The core five principles are Scale, Visual hierarchy, Balance, Contrast, and Gestalt, in no particular order of importance. We will look at these principles and highlight some things to note when designing for our current day.

Contrast

Contrast is the apparent difference between light and dark elements. Simple enough, right. It's just the measure of the difference between saturation levels. The more distinguishable a light element is compared to a dark thing, the higher the contrast. So a blue ball set on a black background has a different contrast to, say, the same ball on a mauve background. In UX design, you want to give essential things higher contrast. Contrast is what leads your eye to buttons and elements that facilitate interaction. The principle of contrast points to the juxtaposition of visually mismatched elements in order to transmit the fact that these elements are different. Contrast is all around us: our choice of clothing is measured against our skin tone to avoid a clash of colors; when we decorate our rooms, we rely on contrast to aid us in determining the best color combination that will bring our imagination to life.

Balance

What happens when elements are off-kilter? What happens when the previous button is misaligned by so little as 5px? How much will that affect the user experience you are shooting for? Balance is simply the distribution of elements in a logical and sensible manner. The elements don't have to be perfectly aligned; that would be boring if you wanted to shake things up. Understanding the fact that balance is one of the reasons behind unique designs, even when the elements seem to overload the design. Striking a balance is an internal thing that comes to maturity the more you experiment and design. Of course, there are principles when it comes to balance, but as you grow and become more proficient, you realize the several paths that are open to you to experiment with. Balance occurs when there exists an equally distributed, not necessarily symmetrical, amount of visual signal on both sides of an imaginary axis.

Scale

In the real world, we perceive things that are close to us more than things that are far away, while in the digital world, bigger things are perceived to be closer while smaller things are perceived to be farther away. Size has a similar effect even if your design looks somewhat *flat*. Digitally, if you use blur effects or shadows, it just makes the perception of depth more realistic; you are replicating how we already perceive things in nature. As a general rule, you want important things to be larger than less important elements. This creates a visual hierarchy on the page and makes it easier to skim through, but it also allows you to decide what the user sees first. That's why it's not a good practice to make the logo bigger unless you want users' attention on your logo instead of buying something. Let's look at a subset of scale:

Repetition and Pattern-Breaking

One crucial visual design principle involves the creation of patterns that nudge the user's eyes toward important things. And like all established rules, patterns are made to be broken. The human brain has a particular talent for patterns and sequences. Whenever something in nature repeatedly happens in cycles, we will tend to notice quickly. In fact, we not only notice these happenings, we think about those things differently. When you line up similar elements, they are perceived as a group, and individuality is lost. If you want these elements to be treated separately, then you must break the pattern – understanding how the brain works is crucial in designing and presenting elements the way you want them to be seen. To make a pattern or a sequence, be sure to keep visual weight and color consistent. Never forget this. The user's eye will begin at one end and follow the pattern laid out to the other end. To break the pattern, simply switch it up in the place where you want to add focus. Example: Make the *Register Now* button an unexpected color, size, shape, or style if you want to bring more attention there.

Be careful: pattern-breaking can lead the user's eyes away from other important things; break patterns with knowledge and caution. If this leading away is what you want, then go right ahead. It should be obvious that you need to make a pattern before you attempt to break it. What does this mean exactly? Simple, establishing a pattern is the first step that will guide how you decide to break it up and for what reason.

Visual Hierarchy

Repetition, as we learned, creates a pattern. However, certain types of repetition can also make the perception of shapes that disrupt where the user's eyes will go. Visual tension is a concept that seems rather basic, but you'd be amazed at how useful it can be. The machine in our heads is a little too good at seeing patterns where they don't exist. As a designer, you can use that. Layout-wise, this can be a wonderful way to put more focus on something small, like a label. Conversely, you can create visual paths leading to the button you want people to click. Vintage ads make use of this technique often to put a small logo into focus. It also conveniently makes a layout feel simpler and more cohesive because a path or a box is only one mental thing. The principle of visual hierarchy lies in guiding the user's eye on the page so that it attends to different design elements in order of their importance. You can also use colors to make a path like a gradient on a list of items. Or you can add visual weightiness to a group of elements by morphing them into one shape instead of separate pieces. This is an absolutely great way to direct the user's attention without adding any more things to a layout.

Gestalt

Gestalt principles capture the totality of our tendency to perceive the whole as opposed to the existing individual elements. It's how the brain perceives and processes things. Gestalt is a German word that translates as a unified whole. Interestingly, there are over ten overlapping principles, with about four or five on the platform of dominance. Laura Busche, the Brand Content Strategist at Autodesk, observes that great designers understand the powerful role that psychology plays in visual perception. What happens when someone sees your design for the first time? How does their mind react to it? Are you sending a message?

The basic law governing a Gestalt principle is that we tend to categorize our experiences in a recognizable, regular, and orderly manner. Pretty much standard behavior if you think about it. This subconscious and orderly perception are what permits us to create meaning out of a complex and chaotic world. You must have found yourself thinking about how the mind works, especially if you have taken psychological tests in the past. Interestingly, you don't have to be a psychologist to use any of the principles that will be mentioned here. Although, having a solid understanding of how these principles work will help you in three ways:

1. At the highest level, the Gestalt principles aid in the design of products that solve the user's problem/meet the user's need in an elegant, pleasing, unencumbered, and intuitive way. Of course, these principles can be used in an unfitting manner, and this doesn't get us what we want. When understanding guides proper usage, the principles don't stress you, the designer, neither does it confuse the user. Without any argument, these principles give you the tools needed to create solutions in record time, thereby giving you more time to lavish on tweaking user experience and making the system better.

2. These psychological principles hold the power to unlocking and influencing how we see the world; there is always a method to the madness. This superpower allows designers to accurately control our attention towards specific elements and areas in the design/system, which in turn guide us to take specific, desired actions, leading to behavioral change or a sale. They essentially give you the same power mentalists have. You become like Poseidon with his trident, willing your users to see what you want them to see, guiding them through the navigation and eventually checkout. Good stuff!

3. These principles will aid you in deciding which design elements will be the most effective in a given situation; knowing which to do away with is also valid. Did you find yourself wondering while reading this chapter about when to use visual hierarchy, background shading, gradients, or how to

group similar items? Gestalt principles give you the ability to know the perfect timing for these things and how to accurately gauge their effect.

Here are seven principles with brief explanations:

1. Figure-ground Principle: The figure-ground principle states that people instinctively perceive objects as either being in the foreground or the background. The elements either stand out prominently in the front, known as the figure – or they recede into the ground(back)

2. Similarity: This principle of similarity states that when things appear to be similar to each other, we naturally group them together. This is a natural reaction that doesn't need any input from you. Interestingly, did you know that we also tend to believe these grouped items have the same function? We absolutely do! A collection of design elements, like color and organization, can be employed to create the illusion of being in similar groups.

3. Proximity Principle: This principle states that things that are brought close together will be perceived to be related than elements that are spaced farther apart from the group. Does this give you an idea about why the spacing is so important? A little pixel to the left, a little nudge of that header, and readability goes out the window. Proximity is incredibly powerful

in that it overrides similarity of shape, color, size, as well as other factors that might distinguish a group of objects.

4. Common region: The popular principle of common region is closely related to proximity; some designers pair them off when making designs. Anyway, it states that when objects are located within the same closed region, we perceive them as being grouped together. Easy right? You have done this a thousand times, but you didn't think much of it. Putting borders or other visible barriers around an image is a great way to create a perceived separation between object groups.

5. Continuity: This principle of continuity states that elements that are arranged on a curve or line will be perceived to be more related than elements not on the line or curve. We like patterns, continuity and it may be something inherited from our ancestors. We immediately recognize the flow of items even when they aren't exactly alike.

6. Closure: This principle states that when we are presented with a complex arrangement of visual elements, we will more than likely look for a single, recognizable pattern among them. In simple and clear terms, when you are presented with an image that has missing parts, your brain goes to work filling in the blanks and turning in a complete image. This is why certain things make sense immediately but may take longer for others. It's the brain's way of making sense of things by

seeking out patterns in everything that doesn't make complete sense at first glance.

7. Focal point: This principle states that whatever dominates visually will capture and hold the viewer's attention first. I feel like we all innately know this without understanding why or the fact that it is a principle. It seems to come with most human OS, this understanding of what will stand out, what colors to use, and all of that. I am not implying that every human on earth is a master color theorist; we have a nudge that we can't explain but those that spend time to understand why this happens are the designers.

In the end, understanding how the mind works is the best place to begin; Gestalt is in the mind, not the eye. Having these principles in your toolkit will greatly improve your ability to pull designs out of seeming thin air.

7

UX Optmization

I've observed over the past years that, in general, there are two different types of UX optimization and two different types of optimizers:

- The first type is typically composed of the big data analysts, the A/B or multivariate testers, and related numbers practitioners. They approach optimization from a quantitative data and metrics analysis perspective. Quantitative data can be thought of as the *what's happening* data. Often qualitative practitioners reside in marketing or product management positions within a firm. This group can flex numbers, and cross-tab spreadsheets like Arnold Schwarzenegger used to flex his biceps.

- The second group is typically composed of the usability and user experience practitioners. This group is generally UX and usability focused types of people interested in qualitative data, like how satisfied a user is, how a user feels about an action, or how easy or difficult it may be for the user to accomplish a task. Qualitative data can be thought of as the *why it's happening* data. This group can analyze qualitative data the way Sigmund Freud analyzed his patients to root out angst about their mothers.

Every group is very good at what they do. The quantitative group can A/B test with the best of them. And the qualitative group can usability test and UX research the hell out of a design. Yet seldom do both groups come together, and seldom does one person do both quantitative AND qualitative as part of their day-to-day role. Thus, quantitative practitioners may know the *what's happening* information associated with the quantitative data of website behavior, but they often don't know the qualitative *why it's happening* side.

Likewise, the qualitative practitioners may know a great deal about the *why it's happening* information associated with the qualitative data, but they often don't know the quantitative *what's happening* side. They don't know what they don't know, and this is precisely why I wrote this book. My goal with this chapter and the next is to help guide you in the ways of combining these two powerful sets of data into a broader, far more robust, and holistic context that improves your ability to analyze and optimize websites and apps.

You will be combining the *what's happening* quantitative data with the *why it's happening* qualitative data to enable much more accurate analysis and subsequent optimization recommendations. If you fall more into the quantitative big numbers group, you will learn what you need to know to apply qualitative data for analysis. And if you fall more into the qualitative group, you will learn what you need to know to apply quantitative big-numbers data and analysis.

Simply put, you will know what you didn't know.

The Four UX Optimization Steps:

1. Defining Personas

Defining and using Personas is the first step in any UX optimization process. That's because you must know who you are trying to improve the website for. Let's face it: it is difficult to admit, but not everyone in the world will find your website or app useful or helpful.

Note: in the interest of more efficient reading, and I'll refer to website optimization for website and app optimization. Just know that all the methods you will use in this book can be applied equally for websites, apps, and systems. Who out there may be interested in the products you offer, service, and website? There's a high probability that it's someone with a NEED your product or service helps address. It's probably someone in need of a solution your business provides. It's probably a person who has this need at a time that causes them to inquire about this product or service immediately. And unless you're selling a $900 million luxury island, the odds are your someone is not alone. There are many, many others who all share that NEED, are SEARCHING for the solution, and are doing it NOW.

Guess what?

All those PEOPLE share several things in common, and because of that, you can group them all together into a single representation called a *Persona*.

You need to use that Persona to help you focus on who you are optimizing the website for. You will use the Personas' needs, their search behaviors and history, and their mental map for how they typically research and find a solution. You will also use other behavioral elements they share to help you understand how your site is performing in helping them achieve their critical tasks. You need Personas because you must analyze the critical tasks necessary for them to be successful on your website. There is a lot to get into regarding personas and how to use them for analysis, in case your firm doesn't use them already. I cannot get into everything because it's beyond the scope of this book.

2. Conduct Behavioral UX Data Analysis

The second step is to conduct behavioral UX data analysis to evaluate the quantitative data associated with Persona activity on your website. Now that you know the Persona and what behaviors they have, you can evaluate those behaviors on your website. This accumulated data is quantitative because it is the what is happening data. You need to analyze the existing user experience of the website based on this quantitative behavioral data. Your goal is to find and evaluate the quantitative data in the context of understanding how your Personas are, or are not, accomplishing their critical tasks. Where is this behavioral UX data gleaned from? Typically it can be in your weblog file analysis systems such as

- Adobe Analytics Cloud

- Google Analytics

- CoreMetrics

- Or related types of website analysis tools

What types of behavioral data do you look at? This will vary depending on the Personas, the type of website you have, and what critical tasks (which come from the Personas) and activities your website visitors are conducting on your site.

Behavioral UX Data Types

In general terms, the most common types of behavioral data you should evaluate in your audit align with fundamental user experience of the site, including

- Conversion Data from ERP & GA Systems

- PPC Keyword Data

- Visits by Browser

- Website Bounce Rate

- Website Conversion Data

- Average Time Spent Per Session and Per Page

- There are others, but it depends on the website and Persona critical tasks

I will drill down into this section in the next chapter, so feel free to skip ahead if you are curious.

So now that you know the types of behavioral UX data you need to audit, you can use that data to have a better sense of *what's happening* on your website. But that's not enough. So what's missing? Although you know what's happening, the behavioral data does not tell you why it's happening. For that, you need to switch to finding and using qualitative data analysis, usability, and UX testing.

3. Conduct UX and Usability Testing

You conduct UX and usability testing to help you uncover the WHY of the behaviors you analyzed in the previous step. You do this by observing real people who match your Personas as they try to accomplish their critical tasks on your website. There are a variety of usability and UX testing tools and data you can use to help you uncover the WHY. The list of what is tools you gravitate towards will vary depending on the Personas, the type of website you have, and what critical tasks and activities your website visitors are conducting on your site. Your goals in conducting the UX and usability testing research is to pinpoint:

- What aspects of the critical tasks work well for your website visitors?

- What does not work well for them?

- Do you have expectations for the experience being met? If yes, why. If not, why not?

- What confuses or causes them concerns?

Types of UX and Usability Testing Data

In the arena of UX testing data, the most common types of data tools should evaluate in your audit align with the critical tasks the Personas are trying to accomplish and may include the following:

- 5 Second Test

- Moderated Usability Test

- Click Test

- Unmoderated Usability Test

- Lesser-known tools that depend on the critical tasks and Persona being considered

In-person or remote moderated usability testing is arguably the richest and most robust way to capture the *why it's happening* data. There are other good methods for obtaining UX and usability testing data, and they include unmoderated usability testing, 5-second testing, question tests, and other types of qualitative UX tests. The UX and usability testing tools above will provide you with the all-important qualitative *why it's happening* data of the quantitative *what's happening* behavioral UX data you already documented. Knowing the *what's happening* data and combining it with the *why it's happening* data, you now have a much clearer picture of the behavior on the site and why that behavior is occurring. What's left to do is to analyze that data, combine it into a set of optimization recommendations, and use them in A/B testing of the website.

4. Analyze Results and Make Recommendations

Next, you combine the analysis of behavioral UX data in step 2 with the UX research and usability testing data from step 3 to determine the *what* and *why* for your website interaction. Your goal is to look for patterns that align with undesirable behaviors. Based on this data, you need to determine where optimization opportunities exist and what changes you believe will improve those behaviors. The quantitative *what's happening* behavioral data is your signpost; you use it to identify where critical tasks are not performing as expected. You will focus on those pages or on those parts of the flow that need attention. The qualitative *why it's happening* data is your tour guide; you use it to identify why those pertinent tasks are not performing as expected. Often those WHY problems may revolve around one of several common usability issues such as those in the next section.

Common Types of Behavioral UX Issues

In general, the most known types of behavioral data you should evaluate in your audit align with fundamental user experience of the website, including:

- Taxonomy not in alignment with users

- Navigation errors or confusion

- Process flow not in alignment with user's mental map

- Other heuristic issues depending on the site

Finally, just because the behavioral UX *what's happening* data and the UX research *why it's happening* data seem to provide you with optimization recommendations, you should never assume that your analysis is correct. My recommendation is that any analysis and set of recommendations always include vetting using A/B testing. A/B testing is the only path to be sure that the optimizations you recommended did, in fact, actually improve things.

8

Behavioral UX DATA

Our present-day means of measuring things are more accurate, but the goal is the same: we measure to prove. Like untrusting sailors testing a cask of rum, we wait to see the flash or fizzle before we declare our success or failure. We currently swim in a sea of data. Quantitative research provides us with a means to navigate it. It measures the world through numerical and statistical analyses. It reports budgets, records populations, and measures speeds. What is the average cost of a U.S. aircraft carrier? Where are women-owned firms flourishing? How long does it take for users to check out? On the surface, such data denotes little information other than numbers.

But further analysis uncovers additional insights. Soaring budgets may signal a rising commodity market. Successful economic zones may indicate a favorable tax policy. Long checkout times may reveal problems with a website's shopping cart. Each measurement quantifies data and shapes our research, proving our success or failure. Where we once guessed people's behavior, we now can track their every click, tap, and swipe. Yet, the research looks backward; we see the wake of the ship, but never what lies ahead. We cannot predict the future with certainty, but what we can do is measure which direction the wind is blowing.

When we delve deeper into quantitative research, we discover that what we are really talking about its significance. Which data aides our decision making and which are merely paper and pixels? A researcher can endlessly record and analyze the world—but to what end? For quantitative research to be useful, it must be practically and statistically significant. Before you jump overboard, know that we will only skim the surface of statistics here. We will cover the basics while avoiding the details that make math professors rejoice and grad students cry. Let us kickoff by defining a few terms. A population is the entirety of a data set, be it a population of English sailors, flying fish, or rum barrels. A population includes every sailor, fish, or barrel— not just the big ones, not just the small ones, not just the ones we want to include; every single one.

Good statistics are generalizable, meaning the statistic can be used to infer conclusions about an entire population. We say the average alcohol proof of a few cups of rum represents the average alcohol proof of all rum barrels. Generalized statistics are not infallible; they do not always lead to exact matches when extending our research across an entire population. Our sample may indicate an average alcohol proof of 74.6, but a few rum barrels might be watered down, while others might put hair on your chest. Reliability describes how often a test produces similar measurements under similar conditions. Testing the height of barrels is reliable, as barrels tend to stay the same height over time. By contrast, rum's color is not reliable because its color fluctuates depending on any number of factors, such as the rum's age and its means of storage. Validity signifies the accuracy of research. From overall conclusions to individual measurements, we want all research efforts to be valid. Truth be told, lighting rum on fire is not an accurate means to measure alcohol content. A modern-day hydrometer would provide a much more valid measurement. But what fun is that?

Luckily, we have many software tools to analyze populations, samples, and statistics. They do much of the work for us. However, knowing how to analyze data allows us to interpret the resulting information and recognize if it is reliable and valid.

Behavioral UX data is the *what's happening* data. Because this data is quantitative by design, it is used to identify what behaviors are, or are not, ongoing on your website. This information is critical for any analysis of website or app optimization opportunities. We use behavioral UX data to determine what types and amounts of interactions are happening on the site or app. This quantitative data, or WHAT data, integrated with the WHY data coming from UX and usability testing gives us a comprehensive outline, or what I refer to as a 360-degree view, into website activity. When analyzed together, the behavioral UX and usability testing data provide a 360-degree view into what's happening and why it's happening on the website. This more educated and enlightened view into website engagement makes for far more informed decisions as to where website issues are, why they are happening, and what to do about them. This leads to better optimization recommendations and improved website conversion.

Behavioral UX data is critical, but by itself, it's not enough to make informed analysis and optimization recommendations. Think about it this way: Behavioral UX data is the sign-post for *what* is happening on a website, but not *why* it's happening.

Sources of Behavioral UX Data

You may be wondering where behavioral UX data come from? Where do we begin sourcing for it and making sense of it all? Patience. I will reveal all in an easy and straightforward manner. There are several common sources for this data, including:

- Website Log Analytics Programs: Google Analytics as an example

- Advertising Systems: Google Adwords, Facebook Ads Manager, or Hootsuite

- Content Management Systems(CMS): WordPress, Drupal, or Magento

- Marketing Automation Systems: Eloqua, Marketo, or Pardot

- eCommerce Systems: BigCommerce, Shopify, Volusion

- Custom Back-End Systems (designed to complete tasks, purchases, transactions)

It can be overwhelming to account for all the possible sources of behavioral UX data. And if you consider all the data available in each of those systems, it can be even excruciatingly overwhelming! The important thing to remember is the aim of using quantitative data from these systems is to help answer specific questions about what's happening in the user experience. What sort of questions you may have and how you use this data is the subject you will explore later in the book. For now, the key point is that once you know your questions, and once you've determined what sort of data you need to answer those questions, it's highly likely that one or several of these data sources will be the place you can go to get that information. Starting with the questions first, and having a sense of the data you need to answer those questions, will reduce that overwhelming feeling you may have due to all that data. And that will make it easier for you to concentrate on the behavioral UX data analysis. Now that you have a fair knowledge of the sources let's look at each of the various types of behavioral UX data available and how they can be used to answer your questions.

Types of Behavioral UX Data

When it comes to analyzing data, Google Analytics is a very popular and widely used analytics platform, and because of that, the reports here will be from that tool. Of course, other web analytics programs like Adobe Analytics exist and have similar reports and data offerings. The brief overview here is only a matter of preference and shouldn't be seen as anything more.

Now, let's get into the bulk of this final chapter. Broadly speaking, there are four types of behavioral UX data, and they are explained below:

Acquisition Data

Acquisition data is useful for determining where people came from when they decided to visit your website or download your app. Knowing where people came from, what they were looking for, and whether they found it (or not) is a critical element of website optimization. The following sections cover several examples of acquisition data and how they can help with optimization.

Organic Search Keyword Data

Organic search keyword data means any keywords people entered and clicked on when they came to your site from the non-paid portion of search results pages. Google and other web analytics tools will provide this information typically in an SEO (Search Engine Optimization) report. Organic search terms are very important for identifying what keywords or phrases people are searching for on search engines when they found your site and clicked to visit. They are also important because they often represent the majority of traffic to a site that converts (i.e., completes an action on the site).

Paid Media Data

Paid media means forms of advertising that are not paid search, such as video ads, display ads, social media ads, and (the still present but almost completely ignored) banner ads. Knowing which paid media ads and the content in those ads your viewers engaged with to visit your site is very helpful contextual *what's happening* data. Much like the organic search data, paid media data can shed light on what concepts, content, or text is triggering a response in your viewers. This data can help you identify what caused visitors to come to your site. Other quantitative data points can be combined with paid media data to determine whether those visitors who clicked a paid media ad stayed on the resulting website page or if they immediately bounced away from that page. Knowing this helps to shed light on whether the paid media ad is properly setting expectations for what content visitors will eventually find, should they click the paid media ad.

Steven Miller

Paid Search Advertising Keyword Data

Paid search keyword data refers to pay-per-click ads, popularly known as PPC, available on search engines such as Google and Bing. PPC ads are the ads on search engine sites that display advertisements in the upper and lower areas of the results pages for keyword searches. Other types of paid search ads include text link ads and related types of paid search-based advertising on sites other than the main search engine sites. Paid search advertising keyword data is very helpful for identifying what terms people were searching for or what they clicked when they came to your site. Among other things, it tells you what specific terms or phrases were being searched for, how many of those terms were entered (impressions), and how many people clicked those terms to visit your site.

Referral Data

A referral is a visit to your website from any referrer source. Referral means "where did your website visitors come from?" Did they come from a search engine through a search results page linking to your site? Perhaps they came from a social media link to your site. Maybe they came from a related topic website. Knowing the referral data about where people came from when they visited your website is another helpful source of *what's happening* data because it provides context to where people were when they came to your site. This is useful information for understanding the context of their visit to your site. Were most visitors coming from a search engine? Were they coming from a competitor's website? Perhaps they were coming from other pages in your site (such as going from an internal page to the home page). Understanding how many visits came from each referral source can help shed light on where visitors came from, where they went on your site, and potentially whether they found what they were looking for or bounced away.

Source/Medium

The Source/Medium Report in Google Analytics is a helpful way to identify which acquisition source and medium are sending traffic to your website. This is useful for identifying how much each of your acquisition channels is contributing toward total traffic to the site and which medium in those sources is providing the visitors. Think of source as the type of channel-like Yahoo, Google, or Bing and the medium as the type of traffic that source is sending; paid, organic, or referral traffic.

Conversion Data

Conversion data is an important behavioral UX data set and is typically what your firm should be obsessed with. Conversion data is used by Support teams, the Marketing, Product, Sales, and to evaluate how efficient the website or app is at attracting and converting visitors into taking various types of actions.

There are many possible types of conversions. Here are just a few:

- Click-Through Rate (CTR): This is a percentage of users who see an ad or link and click it

- Download Rate: The percentage of people who download an app or other file

- Lead Conversion Rate: A catch-all term for any type of conversion that occurs once a lead takes further action on the site, such as downloading a white paper or completing a form

- Lead to Sale Rate: Often used on Business to Business (B2B) websites where the percentage of the number of leads that end up purchasing a product or service is measured

- Shopping Cart Purchase Rate: An important eCommerce metric that measures the number of people who place products in their shopping cart vs. the number who place products in their cart and then actually check out and purchase them

- Suspect-to-Lead Rate: A marketing metric referring to visitors to your website who are initially unidentified but then provide some identification information on a form to become a known "lead"

There are many other forms of conversion data. Most are more specific to the particular needs of the firm in measuring what activity is occurring as a user takes various actions on their website or with their app.

Engagement Data

This section is all about engagement data; a bit on its importance and the various forms it appears as:

All Pages

All Pages is a ranked listing of the pages with the most to least page views for a specific time period. This information can be helpful for identifying pages that users are engaging with and those they are not engaging with. Trending the ranked positioning of a page before and after content or navigation changes can help identify if the optimizations are working by sending more traffic to the page or not.

Behavior Flow

The Google Analytics Behavior Flow Report visually presents the top paths users took from one page to the next. This report is very helpful for visually identifying the most common flow or paths your visitors are taking when engaging with your site. It also helps identify what pages they most commonly visit on their journey on your site.

A Behavior Flow Report is a useful tool for evaluating whether people are taking the desired path to content and by how much. In a perfect world, the top paths you would like your visitors to take would be the most visited pages. Thus in this report, it would be the very top row of pages going from the initial landing page on the left all the way through to the second, third, or potentially fourth interaction on the right. Seeing whether this desired path is or is not displayed at the top in this report is a quick way to determine if your navigation, information architecture, and labeling are working as expected. If a page you are not expecting is ranked in the top row (for example, a search results page in your website), then this may be a bad thing, indicating visitors are unable to find what they are looking for and therefore are searching for it. This often requires further follow-up using qualitative data to determine why your visitors are not finding the information they are looking for.

Bounce Rate

This simply refers to the percentage of visitors who land on a page of your website and then immediately leave your website from that page, also called bounce away, without visiting any other pages. This behavior often occurs if website visitors believe they were going to find certain content when they came to a page on your site, but when they got to that page, they couldn't find the information they came searching for, and so they left your site. In other words, they bounced away. Bounce rate can also help you determine whether your website navigation and labeling are effective or ineffective when directing website visitors to the correct page of content.

Click Heatmaps

A click heatmap is a visual representation that defines where people are clicking on a page. There are a variety of tools that can produce visual heatmaps, including ClickTale, CrazyEgg, and Hotjar. Using one of these tools enables you to determine whether the objects you want visitors to click are working or not. It also shows the objects visitors are clicking that they should NOT be clicking. I've found that graphic design treatments that look like clickable objects but are not often attracted undesired user clicks, which is counterproductive to the user experience. Likewise, if clickable objects are designed such that they do not appear to be clickable, this can cause poorer click activity. The principle that determines whether a graphic image looks clickable or not is known as "visual affordance." This means that the object has a visual appearance that helps a viewer understand the object can be clicked. An example of visual affordance is the blue underlined text on a web page. The blue underline is a visual affordance that we have learned means the text is most likely a hypertext link. Using heatmap data to understand how well visual affordance is or is not working for clickable objects is a great way to hunt down those problematic areas of a design that are causing poor interaction.

Exit Pages and Exit Rate

Exit pages are the last page a website visitor is on before leaving the website. The definition in Google Analytics is the count of the number of pageviews that exited the site from that page. For all the pageviews on a certain web page, the exit rate is the percentage of the page views on that page that was the last page on the website.

Exit rate is different from bounce rate. Bounce rate means only that one particular page was visited before the visitor left the website. With exit page and exit page rate, this implies that other pages were visited on the site prior to the exit from the page in question. High numbers of exits from a page may not necessarily be bad. It's good if that page is the end of a task flow in which the user accomplished their task. It's bad if the exit is in the middle of a task flow, implying users are not accomplishing their tasks.

For example, a high exit rate on the payment confirmation page of an eCommerce website is potentially really good. A high exit rate at the beginning of the checkout process on an eCommerce site is potentially really bad.

Landing Pages

The landing page is a page-specific metric that is useful for counting the number of times visitors first visit a certain page on your website. This is helpful for evaluating whether users are coming to a specific page on your site. The data gotten here can be used over time to evaluate how well audience acquisition campaigns are working in engaging your audience and sending them to a unique page or pages on your site.

Page Depth

This is a high-level metric that is an average of the total number of pages visited per session for a given time period. In theory, a higher number of pages visited per session is associated with a better user experience and engagement with the content. But in fact, this greatly depends on the website and the amount and type of content available. Sometimes it's a good thing for people to only visit one page in a session. For example, if you are sending paid media traffic to a landing page, it would be fine if there was only one page visited. Page session duration and depth will also vary depending on the goals the users have when visiting your site. If you have a publication site with many articles on a subject, you might hope and expect to see more pages visited per session because, in theory, visitors are finding related content they can read about a topic.

Pageviews

Pageviews represent the number of pages being loaded or reloaded in a browser. Pageviews are the total number of page views for all pages in your site for a specified amount of time, such as over a day, week, month, or year. This metric is a high-level metric focused on the total page activity for your site. Remember that a single user can have more than one view of a page during their visit to the site, so higher numbers of page views do not necessarily mean higher numbers of users to the page.

Scroll Heatmaps

Like click heatmaps, scroll heatmaps are a visual overlay of data representing how far down a screen your users scroll. Areas on a page that are viewed more often are displayed with a hot color like red or yellow. Areas on a page that are not viewed often or at all are displayed with a cooler color like green, blue, or no color. Tools like ClickTale, CrazyEgg, and Hotjar offer scroll heatmaps. In the past, there were some heated arguments discussions in the UX field about whether the fold – the area of the page below the browser window – was or was not important. Data from a university study seemed to imply the page fold was actually not important or real because the people who participated in the study actually scrolled well down the page to read the content. To which I say, check out your scroll heatmaps! You may be very surprised at the lack of scrolling people actually do on a page.

Note: that there can be big differences between scrolling on desktop versions of websites vs. mobile versions. Either way, having this scroll heatmap data is a great way to evaluate how much users are scrolling down on your pages and what content they are or are not viewing.

Sessions

A session is a unique set of interactions a single user takes in a given amount of time on your platform. By intentional design, Google Analytics defaults that time frame to 30 minutes. So whatever the user does on your site, such as visiting pages, downloading files, viewing videos, all their interactions in that 30 minute time period are considered a single session. Sessions are a higher-level metric that can help you determine whether activity on your website is going up, down, or staying the same over time.

Another high-level metric is average session duration, which is defined as the total duration of all sessions, measured in seconds, divided by the total number of sessions. This can be a handy way to evaluate how well the content of a website may be engaging the user. Identifying if there are many sessions or pageviews falling within a very brief session duration time period may help identify if visitors are not finding the information they seek or are abandoning the site without exploring additional pages. When trended over time, this data can help identify if content and/or navigation optimizations are having the intended effect of improving the engagement with the site.

Note: In Google Analytics, Google cannot tell how long a visitor stayed on the final page they visited before leaving. There is a technical reason for this that I won't get into in this book. This means session duration could be underreported, sometimes vastly underreported. For trending engagement overtime for the whole site, this is a handy metric, but for unique pages, see the time-on-page metric, which will probably be more useful.

Time on Page

The time on page metric is an average of the total time on that page divided by the total number of page views of that page. As with session duration, Google cannot tell how long someone stayed on the last page of their visit to your site. So as long as this page is not the last page they visited (i.e., has a low exit rate), then this metric will be fairly accurate. Time on page is one of the more useful behavioral UX metrics for evaluating the engagement on a website. Assuming you know how long it takes for the average reader to consume content on the page, you can determine whether your visitors are reading the content or not based on the average time on the page.

A note about time on page: Do not assume pages with higher time on page metrics means those are *better* pages. Remember that pages with little content will produce lower time on page metrics vs. pages with greater amounts of content. So, lower time on page numbers for those pages is actually not a bad thing. Likewise, pages that should have lower time on page numbers but are actually experiencing higher time on page numbers than expected might mean your visitors are having trouble finding what they are searching for.

Users

The users metric is the number of users visiting your website in a specific time period. This is different than sessions in that a single user is only one user, but that user may have more than one session if they come back to the website sometime after the default 30-minute time period has passed. As with sessions, this metric is higher level and helpful for determining how many users are visiting your site, or a page on your site, over a specific time period. Knowing whether this traffic is going up, down, or staying the same is useful for evaluating how well website audience acquisition campaigns are working.

Website Search Keyword Data

Your own website search tool can be a very rich source of data. Assuming you have search capability on your site, you can identify the more common search terms your visitors are entering into your tool when trying to find their desired information. You can also determine the number of times the users find the information and whether they go to the page provided in the search result. This is very helpful for identifying what information your visitors are having trouble finding on your website. Knowing this can help you identify navigation or taxonomy changes that can help improve interaction on your site by making it straightforward and easy for visitors to find the content they seek.

Technical Data

Besides acquisition, conversion, and engagement, the technical information of the user experience on a site can also be an important source of behavioral UX data. Knowing what devices, browsers, screen resolutions, and related technical information the visitors are using are important for evaluating how they are experiencing and interacting with the site. Often, using technical data to identify optimizations can improve the website experience for visitors without having to modify any of the content at all. The following sections cover the more common types of technical data that can and should be evaluated.

Browser and OS

To accurately evaluate the user experience of a website, it is pertinent to know what browsers and operating systems are most commonly used for viewing site pages. The UX of the site should work well for most browsers and operating systems, but the most common browsers should be given special attention to ensure that the experience for visitors using that browser is as optimized as possible. It's careless to make optimization recommendations without first knowing how those changes will impact visitors using your most common browser.

Mobile Devices

This data is helpful for identifying which mobile device or devices are the most commonly used when visiting your site. Knowing this is important for evaluating the experience your visitors are having based on their mobile device type. Optimizing the site for all devices is important, but focusing on the most common devices and ensuring the experience is as good for them as possible is important for maximizing engagement.

The Mobile Overview Report in Google Analytics is helpful for identifying the activity on your site based on the type of device (mobile, desktop, or tablet). Your site should work well across all device types, but ensuring you have the best possible experience for the most common device type is very important.

Page Timings

The Page Timings Google Analytics report is helpful in identifying any pages that are experiencing longer page load times than the average for the site. This data can be used to hunt down poor-performing pages based on page load and then using other data sources to identify what may be causing the poor performance. This data is useful for identifying the pages causing poor load performance.

Screen Resolution

Another important metric to know and use is screen resolution. Knowing how your website looks and acts based on the top screen resolutions can offer insights into why certain user behaviors are or are not happening on the site. When evaluating how to optimize a website or particular page, it's important to ensure a user-friendly experience no matter what size screen the visitor may be using. But be sure to evaluate the page or pages using the most popular screen resolutions to ensure your user experience is as best as possible for that size screen.

Speed Suggestions

A critical element of your website's engagement is the speed with which your pages load. Slower load times have a direct impact on the number of users who tire of waiting for the page to load and end up leaving the site without ever seeing a page. Tracking and optimizing page load speed is a very important aspect of optimizing the user experience of any site. The handy Suggestions Report in Google Analytics identifies by page what speed improvements Google recommend making to improve the load time of the page. This report connects with the Google Page Speed Insights Report that is available separately from Google. You may have to find something similar on whatever platform you differ too, or use Google Analytics if the platform doesn't give you these suggestions and data downpour.

There are other data types, literally hundreds of data element variations, that can be analyzed in order to understand the user. The list presented here isn't exhaustive by any means, but what it does is give you a pad to launch from. Whatever data sources you decide to analyze and use will be dependent on a number of factors ranging from the platform involved, questions asked, and your objective. Behavioral data is crucial towards understanding the user and optimizing the overall user experience and should be treated as such.

CONCLUSION

In the end, we need to have more UX discussions where we do actual work of putting users ahead of whatever system we are attempting to build. If you are building for yourself, then you are the user, and the methods outlined in this book should also help. Of course, you can go ahead to create without using the methodologies addressed in the chapters above, but you do yourself a disservice with this approach; you miss goldmines when proper planning and user consideration is thrown out the window. Going through a UCD approach for your projects helps ingrain those practices into your subconscious, making them second nature. As designers, user experience should be foremost, and the more disciplines you – we – delve into in order to better serve the user, the more successful we become. Designers need more disciplinary crossover because products of today fail to fit into just one medium cleanly. From healthcare, car service to retail, and everything in between, industries are innovating faster and intersecting digital and physical realm. Tesla is an example of a crossover that relies a lot on UX design; carmakers struggled in the past with behavioral decisions to be included. The varying possibilities of choice highlight why it's so crucial for interaction designers and UX professionals to understand industrial design. As we move into the 5th industrial revolution and as the Internet of Things gains more ground, we too will be faced with a situation similar to Donts time, but we will be armed and ready. Anything other than being prepared with theories, practices, and experience needed to move user experience and technology forward will be a failure. I hope that this book has prepared you to explore the realm of UX design and how to get the best to your intended user. Everything covered in this book should give you a strong foundation to launch out, experiment, and create excellent UX. Don't be afraid to make mistakes or falling forward; those are unavoidable and should be treated as a part of life.

See you on the horizon.

About the Author

From when the Internet was a cool word to swing around and crappy UI was the in thing, Steven Miller has been in the game. Slowly picking up wisdom here and there and teaching along the way. When he isn't hunched over his computer pushing pixels around to create amazing graphic and UX, he is traveling or reading travel brochures.

Thank you for reading This Book.

If you enjoyed it please visit the site where you purchased it and write a brief review. Your feedback is important to me and will help other readers decide wheter to read the book too.

Thank you!

Steven Miller